GOLF -
A
POSITIVE
APPROACH

Carol Clark Johnson
National Golf Foundation

Ann Casey Johnstone
Stephens College

GOLF - A POSITIVE APPROACH

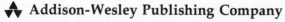 **Addison-Wesley Publishing Company**
Reading, Massachusetts · Menlo Park, California
London · Amsterdam · Don Mills, Ontario · Sydney

ISBN 0-201-03416-6
BCDEFGHIJ-AL-798765

Foreword 1

For many, many years, I have known both Ann and Carol as fellow competitors, teachers and friends. I met Ann when we were both taking lessons from the great teacher, Les Bolstad. We spent hundreds of hours working together and hitting shots. From that time on, we were together often, playing in various tournaments throughout the United States, Britain, Canada, and Europe. I met Carol as a fellow competitor in Westerns and National tournaments in the United States.

I feel that they have extensive background knowledge, playing ability and teaching experience at college, clinic, and individual levels. Ann was voted L.P.G.A. Teacher of the Year for her outstanding teaching and playing abilities, and she has given many National Golf Foundation Clinics throughout the country. Carol has served as area consultant for the National Golf Foundation for seven years and is now the Eastern Educational Consultant, giving many Clinics over the Eastern half of the United States. All of these qualities are necessary to produce a book of advanced material such as this, for use by both teachers and students.

When I have observed their teaching, I've always felt that they both add enthusiasm and zest to their work, because they have such a great love of the game. I know you will find this book with its simple, direct style a benefit to your own game.

With best regards,

Patty Berg
L.P.G.A.
Golf Hall of Fame
Wilson Advisory Staff

Foreword 2

This book is for the serious student of the game. It can be used as a road map in plotting and planning one's individual skill improvement. Written by two knowledgeable and talented L.P.G.A. members, it is filled with tips and suggestions which have been compiled from their many years of experience in teaching and playing. I would recommend it highly to anyone intent on making a strong commitment to the improvement of his own game.

Dr. Gary Wiren
Director of Education
P.G.A. of America

Preface

It's a bright and sunny day. You head for the course full of high hopes for your best *ever* round. You meet your partners and start for the first tee. While taking your practice swing one friend says, "Keep your left arm stiff!" The other one says, "Hold your feet still, keep your eye on the ball, and for heaven's sakes don't kill it—swing easily!"

Certainly your friends mean well. But they have just about ruined your chances of ever hitting a ball well. The slow-swing theory alone will help only one person—your opponent—because he's going to out-drive you!

In the years that we have been around golf, we have heard many cliches and seen many good and bad approaches to the game. Through our teaching, we have found a need for a book designed for advanced players, students and teachers. It must be practical and simple in approach, but one complete to the extent that it not only covers the basic components of the modern golf swing but also goes into the details necessary for making advanced and more complicated shots.

Beginners can use the basic material, but it is beamed for the player who has been on the course and has played a reasonable amount of golf. In the basics, we have covered the grip, stance, full swing, short shot, sand shot, and putting. (In all cases, explanations are made with a right-handed player in mind.) In the more advanced level, we have included various lies and trouble shots, advanced sand shots, coaching suggestions, game analysis, and suggestions for introspection of your mental attitude. In a nutshell, we have covered the mental and physical aspects of the game in advanced detail. For your special information, we have included safety, equipment, rules and courtesies, and a look at tournaments and future careers available to you in golf.

We want to present the modern golf swing in its simplest form. We have started with analyzation, because we feel that once you know how to make the basic moves, you are then ready to seek another level of learning. We want you to inspect your mental approach by knowing yourself. We hope you will then analyze your game physically and go to each chapter that will help you improve.

Just as one of our basic hopes of the book is to encourage you to look at yourself, we also have looked at our approach to the game. We try to teach in a simple, concise method that eliminates the prose of talking. We both try to use word pictures and simple check points on grip, stance, and execution, to give you, the reader, a clear picture of what we are saying. We want you to be able to take this book to any part of the golf course or practice range, look up the shot you want, and find out how to execute it. You will then be able to practice the moves without reading long paragraphs of explanation. Teachers can assign a chapter or shot to a class. Students can work at their own pace to learn a specific shot.

Our hope is to help you improve your game, for through better golf, you will have a greater enjoyment of the game that has brought such unmeasurable pleasure into each of our lives.

Cincinnati, Ohio   C.C.J.
Columbia, Missouri   A.C.J.
January 1975

Acknowledgments

We both wish to express our thanks to Guest Author G. Jean Cerra, for her scientific thoughts on the golf swing which make up all of Chapter three.

We are indebted to the National Golf Foundation and the opportunities it offered through seminars, clinics, and staff meetings, and especially to Jim Flick and Bill Strausbaugh for their inspiration to study; to Bullet and Peggy Kirk Bell and Pine Needles for sharing "paradise"; to Patty Berg as a friend and fellow competitor; to Dr. Katherine Ley, who told us to get going and write it all down; and to Caryl Newhof, our direction pointer.

Our thanks go the many students who have inspired our work. We are especially grateful to the golfers who posed for the pictures throughout this book—Donna Jo Rogers, Jorgene Barton, Vee Ann VanPatten, Gail Hollowell, Mike Gill, Larry Stone, Monica Ralph, Gene Neff, Jimmy Martin, Bill Martin, Les Johnstone, Mary Martin, Patty Berg, Jeannie Johnstone—and to photographers, Linda Bell Upton, Lee Ann Maguian, and Merry Martin. Special thanks go to Beatty Wharton, idea and structure guide; to Sandy Finkebeiner and her typing fingers; and to our editor, typist, and friend, Jane Scheele, for her diligent hours of deciphering.

We would like to acknowledge the contributions of the following people who have not only helped us with our book but also have served as inspirations in our golfing careers: For Ann, thanks go to her great golf instructor, Les Bolstad, University of Minnesota golf coach; to her family, the Caseys; to her husband and daughter, Les and Jean Ann, for their patience and understanding; and to Stephens College, and to her Chairwomen, Wilma D. Haynes and Dorothy L. Jones. For Carol, thanks go to her professional, Bob Gutwein, who made the game such challenging fun that the work became easy; to her family, the Clarks, who presented her with all opportunities; to Jim, Jan, Sal, Jay, Carrie, and Jimmy, for patience and push; to Larry Shute for assistance; to General Electric Park; to Greenhills Country Club; and to Coke's Athletic Council, the medium.

Contents

1
What Do You Know About Yourself and Your Golf Game?

The mechanical movements of the golf swing have been explored in such detail in the past few years that it is relatively easy to find almost all the answers to the questions of how, why, and the when of various golf moves. However, after you have decided on those moves that suit your understanding and desires to hit the ball, applying them to the course and under competitive situations adds another dimension to the game. The questions always arise—what makes a champion or an outstanding player? What makes his game outstanding? Why is one player with such gifted mechanical moves falling short of the less talented player who seems to score better with far less talent?

You have now launched into the most difficult aspect of golf. The understanding of the psychological aspects of sports and performers in general is, of course, a reasonable approach.

In order to help you understand these areas, an extensive list of articles and books have been added to the end of this chapter for further research. But what can you do to better understand yourself, your approach, and your behavior under these circumstances? The old cliche, "know yourself," is a good starting point. Know your strengths and weaknesses. Know the good parts of the game you have, and know your enemies—the poor parts.

Some of our prominent golf professionals have on their required reading lists for their students such books as *The Power of Positive Thinking*, *Psycho-Cybernetics*, *I'm OK, You're OK*, and *Born to Win*. The basic thoughts in these books and in others like them are the positive approaches to problems, the programming of positive thoughts.

For the purpose of understanding the psychological performances of athletes, the Institute for the Study of Athletic Motivation has been established at San Jose State College in California. It was organized by Dr. Bruce C. Ogilvie and Dr. Thomas A. Tutko. They have tested more than

1

ten thousand athletes on their personality traits by the use of motivational profiles. An individual or members of a team can be tested by the Institute for a nominal fee.

Emotional Traits

One of the current tests includes approximately 190 questions testing the following eleven areas of drive or emotional traits.

Drive.   Desires to win or to be successful; aspires to accomplish difficult tasks; sets and maintains high personal athletic goals; responds positively to competition; desires to attain athletic excellence.

Aggressiveness.   Believes one must be aggressive to win; releases aggression easily; enjoys confrontation and argument; is sometimes willing to use force to achieve an end; will not be pushed around; may seek to revenge an apparent injury.

Determination.   Is willing to practice long and hard; works on skills until exhausted; often works out willingly alone; perseveres, even in the face of great difficulty; is patient and unrelenting in work habits; doesn't give up quickly on a problem.

Guilt-Proneness.   Accepts responsibility for personal actions; accepts blame and criticism even when it is not deserved; tends to dwell on mistakes and to punish him or herself for them; is willing to endure much physical and mental pain; will play even when injured.

Leadership.   Enjoys the role of leader and may assume it spontaneously; believes he or she is viewed by others as a leader; attempts to control his or her environment and to influence or direct other people; expresses opinions forcefully.

Self-Confidence.   Has unfaltering self confidence in his or her capacity to deal with things; confident of powers and abilities; handles unexpected situations well; makes decisions confidently; speaks up for beliefs to coaches and players.

Emotional Control.   Tends to be emotionally stable and realistic about athletics; is not easily upset; will rarely allow feelings to show and does not allow performance to be affected by them; is not easily depressed or frustrated by bad breaks, calls, or mistakes.

Mental Toughness.   Accepts strong criticism without feeling hurt; does not become easily upset when losing or playing badly; bounces back quickly from adversity; can take rough coaching; does not need excessive encouragement from the coach.

Coachability. Respects coaches and the coaching process; is receptive to coaches' advice; considers coaching important to becoming a good athlete; accepts the leadership of the team captain; cooperates with authorities.

Conscientiousness. Likes to do things as correctly as possible; tends to be exacting in character, is dominated by sense of duty; does not try to "con" the coach or fellow players; does not attempt to bend rules and regulations to suit personal needs; places the good of the team above personal well being.

Trust. Accepts people at face value; believes what the coach and teammates say and does not look for ulterior motives behind their words or actions; is free of jealous tendencies; tends to get along well with teammates.

Tests such as these can help you to better understand yourself and to see how these traits relate to your performance on the course.

The chapters that follow are an attempt to help you improve your skills and broaden your base of understanding of some of the more intricate parts of the golf game. We have prepared some thought-provoking questions to help you to become aware of yourself and your approach to your game, to see your strong points, and to recognize your needs to improve.

General Thoughts

1. Take a total look at your approach to golf.

2. Figure out why *you* want to play golf.

3. Think about your swing.

    A. Are the moves mysterious to you?

    B. Do you understand the mechanical moves but still fail to score well under actual play?

    C. Do you make things complicated or simple?

4. Break the game down into parts, analyze yourself and your performance, and then decide which parts of the game appeal to you the most.

    A. Which parts do you perform the best?

    B. Which ones do you practice the most and why?

5. How do you play when it really means something to you?

6. How do you stand up under the emotional strain of the game?

7. How do you handle the emotions of competition?

During the Game

1. Do you win the tough ones?
   A. Do you fall short under the desire to win?
   B. Do you play better when challenged?

2. When you stand ready to hit a shot:
   A. Do you plan how you want the shot to go?
   B. Do you see all of the trouble out in front of you?
   C. Does the trouble distract you from your shot?

3. When you stand over a putt:
   A. Do you see and feel the putt, its line, its distance, and the ball dropping into the cup?
   B. Do you see yourself missing the putt before you hit it?
   C. Are you thinking of the mechanical moves of the putt?

4. Do the shots seem easier some days than others?

5. Do you play offensively or defensively on the course?

6. Do you enjoy match play? Do you enjoy stroke play?
   A. Do your mechanical moves hold up?
   B. Do you feel confident that you can do the job or do you rely on luck?

7. Can you concentrate on the job to be done?
   A. Do you play stroke by stroke,
   B. hole by hole,
   C. match by match?

8. Do you play the round mentally before the actual game?
   A. Do you use strategy involving your opponent?
   B. Do you visualize good shots or bad shots being made?

9. Do you let bad shots bother you?
   A. Do you go onto the next shot trying to improve?
   B. Do you dwell on your last mistake?

10. Do you concentrate on where the shot is going to go or how your swing will work?

During Practice

1. Do you have short term goals?
2. Do you work on one phase of your swing at a time?
3. Do you think of your swing in simple moves and parts?
4. Can you weed out the excess in your swing and stick to the basics?
5. Do you follow the instructions of your teacher or do you try it your way?

Summary

The whole purpose of this book is to show you the mechanical moves that produce the soundest way to hit a golf ball. Whether thinking about your game in general, on the course, or during the practice session, your major job will be to know yourself. By applying your strengths and knowing your weaknesses, the end result should produce a more positive approach to the game and a vastly improved enjoyment of golf. Never stop striving to know the physical and mental aspects of the game.

Bibliography

Cratty, Bryant J., *Movement Behavior and Motor Learning*, 2nd. ed., Philadelphia, Pa.: Lea & Tebiger, 1969.

Cratty, Bryant J., Miroslav Vanek, *Psychology and the Superior Athlete*, University of California at Los Angeles, Calif.: The Macmillan Company, 1970.

Frost, Reuben B., *Psychological Concepts Applied to Physical Education and Coaching*, Reading, Mass.: Addison-Wesley Publishing Company, 1971.

Kenyon, Gerald S. (Ed.), *Contemporary Psychology of Sports*, Procedures of the 2nd International Congress of Sport Psychology.

Moore, J. W., *The Psychology of Athletic Coaching*. New Haven, Conn.; South Connecticut State College, Minneapolis, Minn, Burgess Publishing Company.

Quest VI, "A Symposium on Motor Learning," National Association of Physical Education and Health of College Women, National Association of Physical Education and Health of College Men, Monograph VI, Spring Issue, May 1966.

Quest XIII, "Psychology of Sports," Monograph XIII, Winter, January 1970.

Richards, Jack W., and Thomas Tutko, *Psychology of Coaching*, Boston, Mass.: Allyn and Bacon Inc., 1971.

Sage, George S., *Introduction to Motor Behavior, A Neuropsychological Approach*, Reading, Mass.: Addison-Wesley Publishing Company, 1971.

Sage, George H. (Ed.), *Sport and American Society*, Reading, Mass.: Addison-Wesley Publishing Company, 1970.

Singer, Robert N., *Motor Learning and Human Performance Application of Physical Skills*, New York, N.Y.: The MacMillan Company, 1968.

2
Game Analysis

Your golf swing is the one part of your golf game that you will try to keep the same. Courses, weather, emotions, and playing conditions change every day, but hopefully your golf swing remains constant. Spend time making it sound! As well as spending time working on your swing, take a look also at your over-all performance on the course. By using the charts in this chapter and practice analyzations of your playing, you should be able to find those areas that need work and concentration. You will be able to plan more meaningful practice sessions and rounds of golf which should, in turn, help you lower your scores.

Course Analysis

1. *Score graph* (Fig 2.1) Similar to a stock market graph.

   A. Record your score each time you play so that you can see your progress.

2. *Shot record* (Fig 2.2) Record the number of putts, chip shots, drives, second shots, slices, hooks, rough shots, and sand shots taken. This will give you a running account of how you played the round.

3. *Plan strategy*

   A. Analyze your strengths and weaknesses using these charts.

   B. Set goals for practice and play.

      i) Practice to strengthen your weak areas.

      ii) Practice to improve your trouble holes.

      iii) Practice with clubs most used on a specific course.

PROGRESS CHART
(Sample)

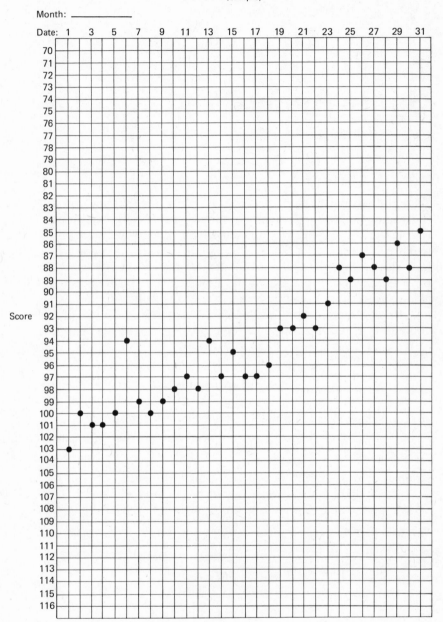

◀ **Fig. 2.1** Score graph

GOLF COURSE _____ WEATHER CONDITIONS _____

TYPE OF COMPETITION _____

Holes	Par	Total strokes	Green in regulation	Number of putts	Drive in fairway	Approximate distance	Club to green	Chip, pitch, or sand	Length first putt
1									
2									
3									
4									
5									
6									
7									
8									
9									
out									
10									
11									
12									
13									
14									
15									
16									
17									
18									
in									
total									

Explain (1) Three Putts   (2) Double Bogies

No. of Birdies _____ _____

No. of Bogies _____ _____

Fig. 2.2 Shot record

STEPHENS COLLEGE
GOLF SCORING SHEET

U. of Cincinnati vs. Stephens

Date: 4-23-74   At: U. of Cin.

Name	1	2	3	4	5	6	7	8	9	out	10	11	12	13	14	15	16	17	18	in	total
Susan Rives	5	7	5	6	5	6	4	4	6	48	6	8	6	5	6	9	5	5	7	57	105
Kim Peterson	5	6	5	5	5	6	6	5	5	48	6	6	4	5	7	7	5	4	5	49	97
Bonnie Dennison	6	7	6	4	5	6	7	4	5	50	6	8	5	5	6	6	6	4	5	51	101
Carol Anderson	6	6	5	4	6	7	5	4	5	48	7	11	5	5	6	10	5	6	7	62	110
Kerry Davidson	8	7	6	4	5	7	5	4	5	51	4	6	7	5	7	7	6	4	6	52	103
																			5	1	6
Par	5	5	4	4	4	5	4	3	4	38	4	5	4	4	5	5	4	3	4	38	76

RECAPITULATION

Fig. 2.3 Team score sheet

4. *Team play*

   A. Keep records of the team as a whole (see Fig. 2.3); it will indicate the holes on which most of the team has difficulty and show the type of practice or strategy needed.

Hole Analysis

1. *Par*

   A. Using your box score, check the number of pars, birdies, and bogies you have made.

GOLF SCORE ANALYSIS SHEET

NAME: _____ _____
         (last)   (first)

COURSE: _____

DATE: _____ .

Hole	1	2	3	4	5	6	7	8	9	out	10	11	12	13	14	15	16	17	18	in	total
Par																					
Score																					
+ or −																					
Errors:																					
#1 wood																					
Fairway wood																					
Long iron																					
Medium iron																					
Short iron																					
Chip																					
Pitch & run																					
Putt																					

RECAP: (total errors   COMMENTS:
for each type shot)   _____

#1 wood   _____   _____
Fairway wood _____   _____
Long iron   _____   _____
Short iron   _____   _____
Chip   _____   _____
Pitch & run   _____   _____
Putt   _____   _____

Fig. 2.4 Personal game-analysis sheet

B. If you are a beginner, set up your own standards for par.
   i) Beginners: Shoot for 8's and 7's on each hole.
   ii) Intermediate players: Shoot for 7's and 6's.
   iii) Advanced and accomplished players: Shoot for 5's and pars.

2. *Scorecard analysis*
   A. Keep records of your own scorecards (Fig. 2.4) and determine on
      which holes additional practice is needed.

hole	hdcp.	yards	champ.	par					par	yards
PLEASE KEEP CARTS ON PATHS, REPLACE ALL DIVOTS and OBSERVE GOLF ETIQUETTE								LADIES PAR		
1	8	520	552	5					5	420
2	14	381	411	4					4	341
3	18	182	208	3					3	115
4	10	384	413	4					4	284
5	2	414	448	4					4	337
6	9	401	434	4					4	305
7	7	528	565	5					5	452
8	16	178	218	3					3	150
9	4	404	440	4					4	329
OUT		3392	3689	36					36	2733
10	1	424	452	4					4	344
11	3	549	574	5					5	455
12	15	350	393	4					4	310
13	11	371	407	4					4	316
14	5	532	568	5					5	442
15	13	377	412	4					4	312
16	12	195	224	3					3	125
17	6	401	432	4					4	312
18	17	185	222	3					3	155
IN		3384	3684	36					36	2771
TOT.		6776	7373	72					72	5504
HDP.										
NET										

Scorer _____ Date _____

Attest _____

◀ **Fig. 2.5** Score card

B. Study the card and play the course mentally, determining which clubs you will use and how you will hit each shot; keep in mind the lie, terrain, wind, and weather conditions.

C. Check the handicap column on the score card (Fig. 2.5) to see which holes are the hardest to score par.

  i) The holes are arranged in order of difficulty to score par, with number 1 being the hardest and number 18 the easiest; every scorecard should have a handicap column.

Playing Strategy

1. *Chart the course*

  A. Use landmarks to measure distances from the tee to the green.

   i) Check for 150-yard markers, trees, or bushes from the green.

   ii) Know the size of the greens.

    a) Know the distance from front to back and the width, side to side, of each.

    b) Check the grain of each green.

  B. Know how far you hit each of your clubs.

  C. Know the prevailing and daily wind directions.

  D. Watch weather conditions:

   i) temperature—ball goes farther in warm weather;

   ii) humidity—ball goes farther in dry weather.

  E. Ground conditions:

   i) Ball goes farther when ground is hard.

   ii) Types of soil

    a) The ball goes farther on clay base soil.

    b) The ball gets less roll on sand base soil.

  F. Check to see how the tee is aligned to the fairway:

   i) Tee the ball on the teeing ground on the side of the trouble, aiming and hitting away from the trouble.

    a) Trees on the right side—tee on the right side of the tee.

2. Club selection

  A. Choose the club that will hit the ball to a specific spot.

    i) From the tee, choose the club that will put the shot in the most advantageous spot for the second shot.

      a) From the tee use a driver or drive with a higher numbered wood or an iron to set up the position for the second shot.

    ii) Choose the position for the second shot to land.

      a) Use irons in the fairway, rough, or hazard, if necessary, to produce best position.

      b) A cardinal rule: choose the club for the lie first, distance second.

      c) Aim shots for the middle of the green.

  B. Play the safest shot. When you figure a shot, try to determine what your percentages are to make the shot:

    i) Check to see if there are any openings through the branches of the trees.

    ii) Know the height of the club chosen. Don't try to make the club perform a miracle.

    iii) Play a lay-out or safety shot short of trouble, such as a creek, trap, dog-leg; don't go from bad to worse.

  C. Short shots

    i) Analyze the situation and think of different ways to perform the shot; choose the shot that you feel will be the most accurate for you to execute.

    ii) See the short shot diagram (Fig. 2.6).

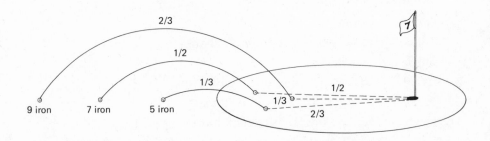

Fig. 2.6 Short shot diagram

D. On the Green

    i) Normally use your putter.

    ii) When putting from the edge of the green, when the ball is lying right next to the fringe, consider using a 3-, 4-, or 5-iron in place of a putter.

    iii) When you are not able to get relief under the normal rule, or on a dog-leg-shaped green, use a 7-, 8-, or 9-iron or a wedge to chip the ball over a casual water spot.

    iv) On extremely large greens, your judgment of a long distance shot may be somewhat off. Such shots are better executed using a 3-, 4-, or 5-iron in place of the putter.

3. *Dog-legs and trouble areas*

A. Play shots away from trouble.

B. Play the shortest way to the green when possible.

C. Play a practice round to check the following:

    i) tee alignment to target;

    ii) creek placement (or know the carry of the ball over water);

    iii) thickness of woods, density of rough, and the type of grass in the rough;

    iv) placement of traps, texture, and difference of sand;

    v) placement of stakes and distance to out of bounds;

    vi) types, elevations, and rolls on the greens;

    vii) prevailing wind direction.

3
Scientific Analysis of the Golf Swing

G. JEAN CERRA

Some disagreement has been expressed as to whether or not the golf swing falls into the category of a sidearm (e.g., tennis, softball) or underhand (e.g., bowling, hockey drives) movement pattern. Many feel that because the ball is on the ground and the swing is mainly vertical as opposed to horizontal, that it should be considered as an underhand pattern of movement. Others feel, however, that the position of the golf club, when stopped at the top of a full backswing, as well as the stance and weight distribution, closely parallels that of a bat in the ready position. Electromyography (a tracing very similar to that of an electrocardiogram which shows the changes in action potential produced by muscular contractions) has revealed that there is much similarity between golf and batting in the way muscles function in these two activities.[1] Another point golf and batting have in common is that two hands are used to control the implement, whereas many sidearm activities require the use of only the dominant hand.

The main objective in the golf swing, as in any striking activity, is to transfer the power from the club to the ball. Again, in this respect, batting and the golf swing are similar. However, in most respects, even though the ball is smaller, golf becomes the simpler of the two. In golf the ball is stationary and therefore the problems in batting associated with speed the ball is traveling, the spin on the ball, and the height at which the ball is to be contacted do not have to be considered or adjusted to during the golf swing. The basic problem in golf is how the desired amount of force is going to be produced and applied to the club and directed by the clubhead through the center of the ball and in the desired direction. Many of these important factors are directly dependent on the actions of the golfer, but many have already been controlled by the manufacturer of the club.

Each club is designed to be of a different length and each clubface has a different pitch or angle. This results respectively in differences in distance and trajectory the ball will travel. If we assume that all clubs are the same length and that only the angle of the clubface is different for the 14 clubs, and that all 14 clubs were swung at the identical rate of speed (all other factors being equal), we would find that the distance the ball would travel would be inversely or *indirectly* proportional to the angle of the clubface; i.e., the greater the angle of the clubface, the less the distance. This is simply the principle of angle of incidence equaling angle of rebound or reflection. So long as each club strikes the ball squarely with its face in a natural position, each will project the ball at a different angle.

Now let us assume that the reverse is true; that is, that the angle of the clubface is constant for all 14 clubs and only the length of the club or shaft varies. If we again swing the clubs at an identical rate of speed and keep all other factors equal and constant, we would see that the distance the ball travels in this instance is *directly* proportional to the length of the club; i.e., the longer the shaft, the greater the distance. The length of the shaft regulates the linear speed of the clubhead. Given the fact that all clubs are swung through approximately the same size arc in a full swing, due to a longer shaft or radius, the longer club has to travel a greater distance in the same amount of time as the shorter club and therefore has to travel at a greater speed.

Golf equipment has been designed with the above two principles in mind and as a result there is no need for the golfer to have to alter his swing in order to achieve the desired results. The longer shaft is attached by the manufacturer to the clubface with the least angle and therefore two of the needed criteria for greater distance are joined together to produce the maximum distance. The golfer simply has to choose one club or another, depending on the distance or height desired.

As a result of these fixed factors being built into the equipment, the problem in golf becomes mainly one of *control*. Each swing can be executed with the same force and in the same plane. The extra length in the club however, although bringing about more force, makes control of the clubhead much more difficult than it would be for shorter implements used in batting or other sports. If it were not for the help of gravity gained in a vertical type swing, it would be practically impossible to control this length of club in a striking activity. Added to this is the problem of a small striking surface which makes accuracy of contact a major concern. The problem then is to *groove* the swing into a certain plane and to put together a sequence of movements which will produce the optimum amount of force each time. Advanced players, having greater control of the club, do adjust the swing as well as the position of the clubface and stance, thereby giving them many more than 14 possibilities for ball flight and distance.

Now let us examine what you, the *golfer*, can do to produce this control and optimum amount of force. Since the ball is stationary, no force is available from the momentum of the ball as is the case in tennis or softball. All the force applied is dependent on the speed at which the clubhead is moving at impact and on the accuracy of contact; that is, whether the force is applied through the center of gravity of the ball.

Grip

In any of the three principal methods of gripping a golf club, certain mechanical disadvantages exist. Both hands are placed on the club so that their actions oppose each other; that is, while the top hand is pushing back, the bottom hand is pulling back. Also, due to the muscular structure of the hand and arm, a grip using mainly the fingers eliminates much of the available force produced by wrist action. The reason for this is that the muscles which close the fingers originate in the forearm and have their tendons crossing the wrist to the fingers. These same muscles have the secondary function of flexing the wrist. Anytime then that the fingers are closed, as around the grip of a golf club, a great deal of the movement possible in these tendons is lessened. What this means is that the tighter one grips the club, the less the hinging mobility of the golfer at the wrist or the degree of flexion he can attain. To a lesser extent this affects the ability to *cock* or *uncock* the wrist (movements perpendicular to that of flexion and extension). This combination of tightness and mobility is something which each golfer must derive in order to meet the needs of his or her own swing. Some hinging is necessary in order to reproduce the lower hinge in the "two-lever principle"[2] to be discussed later.

The way the hands are placed on the club also affects the hinge. The need to get the shaft to form as nearly as possible a straight continuation of the left arm will dictate to a large extent the hand position. Placing the top hand too far over to the right and the bottom hand under the grip allows the forearms to *roll* more and at the top of the backswing the hands are in a freer position to *cock*. This is due to the fact that the hands in this position are in semipronated and semisupinated positions, making complete pronation and supination only a quarter movement away. This position may give a weaker player more of a sensation of being able to lash the clubhead through the ball, but it also complicates the danger of mistiming. Placing the hands in the proper position with the fingers diagonal to the shaft of the club puts the meat part of the hand behind the club and in a better position to add power to the swing.

Which of the three grips is the best to use from the standpoint of mechanics is a debatable point. Just because many of the world's best golfers use the overlapping grip, does not necessarily mean that it is the best grip for those weaker golfers who lack the physical make-up to be first class players. Bunn[3] analyzed the striking movements of the hands and felt that since a fulcrum or pivot point is located between the center of the hands, "the further the hands are spread, within practical limits of course, the greater the power of the stroke" (Ref. 3, p. 230). It is assumed that Bunn is considering the more traditional type swing or what Cochran and Stobbs refer to as the *"free 'roller' — open-at-the-top"* method[2]. Bunn suggested that this would indicate that a grip where the hands are not joined together in any way, as in the *baseball* or *ten-finger* grip, would be best to use for individuals lacking terrific wrist power. Many women fall into this category. Out of the 18 subjects he tested, he found that 50% got more force into their swing by using the "baseball" grip[3]. No mention, however, was made regarding accuracy of contact using this type of grip.

A study by Walker[4] however revealed opposing results. After comparing the performances of 24 male golfers who used each of the three grips, he found that no one of the grips was statistically superior to either of the others, in terms of greater distance or accuracy.

Other authors[5,6,7] have indicated, contrary to Bunn's wrist-action-supplying-power theory, that the greatest force which can be developed with a given amount of body power is centrifugal in nature. This would best be accomplished when the hands act as a unit rather than separately. The overlapping or interlocking grips, because the hands are in contact, make this easier. Broer[1] suggests that although it is possible for some individuals to control the wristy action of the hands suggested by Bunn and to take advantage of any extra force thus produced, others might find that the baseball grip leads to loss of control and that they are able to generate more *controlled* force through the use of one of the other two grips.

Stance

The placement of the feet relative to one another and to the intended direction of the ball plays an important role in determining both the speed of the clubhead when it meets the ball and the desired direction in which the ball is to travel. The stance makes it possible to use the entire body in the swing by transferring the weight from the back to the forward foot.

Stance is also important from the standpoint of equilibrium. One basic mechanical principle states that the wider the base of support, the more stable the object. However, in golf it is possible to attain a stance that is so wide that the freedom with which a player can use the muscles of the legs and hips in the power generation sequence is restricted. A stance that is too wide stops the player from turning fully and, by doing this, prevents the strong muscles in the legs from being fully utilized for the desired pulling action.

The converse is also true. A stance that is too narrow, that is one with the feet together, inevitably makes the golfer conscious of the narrowness of his or her base and of the need to maintain balance. The golfer's attention is consequently diverted to this rather than focused on the primary objective—that of imparting the necessary force to the ball. Just as too wide a stance inhibits using the strong leg muscles properly, a stance with the feet too close together also prevents using the leg drive as a source of power to produce lateral movement of the hips and lower torso.

How one places the feet relative to the intended line of flight, i.e., "open," "closed," or "square," also affects the desired direction of the ball and will also depend to some extent on the intent of the shot, i.e., hook or slice, and on the length of the shot required, i.e., distance or accuracy. The section on stance (Chapter 5) illustrates how stance affects the hooking or slicing action of the ball. Stances with either foot drawn too far back from the intended line of flight can make it more difficult for the golfer to keep his swing along the line to the target, thereby sacrificing control. A closed stance, for instance, allows the golfer greater freedom to pivot and generate maximum power on the backswing, but reduces the freedom of body action on the follow-through.

Very little evidence exists relating to which stance is superior to the others for those shots requiring maximum or near-maximum effort. However, where accuracy rather than distance is the prime consideration, a somewhat open stance tends to restrict the range of the backswing and thereby decreases one's chance for error without sacrificing or preventing the desired force from being generated[8].

In any case, extremes in openness, closeness, width, or distance from the ball should be avoided since they will lead to loss of power and consistency. Cochran and Stobbs[2] found that an analysis of 14 top professional golfers revealed that, on the average, they stood for drives with their feet 24½ inches apart and with the toes square to the line of flight. This does not mean that this measurement is ideal for every golfer because differences in size and height of the golfer affect the width of the stance. Therefore, a stance approximately hip width apart is recommended.

Strokes for Distance

The speed with which the clubhead is moving is an important factor in determining the force imparted to the ball. The problem is for golfers to coordinate into one smooth sequence the use of their muscles and the leverage supplied by their arms to bring about the desired speed.

The movements in any driving or distance stroke are principally rotatory (involving rotation about an axis) in nature. The only linear movement is the lateral movement which initiates the downswing, moves the center of gravity forward, and shifts the weight from the rear to the forward foot. The rotation takes place along the long or vertical axis of the body (from center of the head, through the spine, and down between the feet). In order to prevent any displacement of this axis resulting in a "swaying" error and inaccurate contact with the ball, the head is held as stationary as possible and the heel of the forward foot is held on the ground as long as possible in order to hold this axis in a relatively fixed position.

The purpose of the backswing is to put the golfer and the club into the optimum position from which to start the downswing. Carrying the clubhead straight back low to the ground as far as possible flattens the arc of the swing and thus aids accuracy of contact. As mentioned earlier in the section dealing with equipment factors affecting greater force, the longer the club, the greater the distance. The same is true of the golfer's arms: keeping the front arm relatively straight gives a longer radius and therefore a longer lever. Combining the length of the arms to that of the clubs, the length of the radius is increased even more. This longer radius results in the clubhead being capable of a greater velocity since the clubhead travels through a longer arc in a given amount of time and therefore moves faster. (See Fig. 3.1.)

The length of the backswing directly affects the length of the arc. The longer this arc, the more time available to build up momentum. Hay[8] suggests that "the end of the backswing is reached with the hands at or slightly above head height, the upper trunk rotated approximately 90° from its original position, and the wrists cocked so that the club shaft lies over and behind the head at some 0 to 45° above the horizontal" (Ref. 8, p. 279). If the backswing is so long that the clubhead drops below the horizontal, it must be raised *against* the force of gravity as the downswing begins and results in a *flinging* or *throwing* action of the hands at the top, disrupting the pulling action of the left side. Control is made more difficult and the club is likely to take a position ahead of the hands on the downswing.

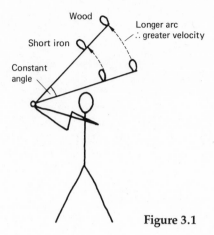

Wood
Longer arc
∴ greater velocity
Short iron
Constant
angle

Figure 3.1

The long backswing necessitated by shots for distance brings into play more muscles which can contribute to the swing and therefore can generate more force. The long radius and arc place those muscles of the left or target side on maximum stretch. The greater the stretch, the greater the distance over which the muscles can contract and thereby produce more force. The muscles of the back and shoulder girdle work in opposition to each other during the backswing and at the initiation of the downswing. Those muscles which actively bring about the *pushing action* to initiate the backswing are primarily located on the left anterior and right posterior sides of the shoulder girdle (for a right-handed golfer). Those muscles located on the back of the left arm and shoulder girdle, including the back left side of the back, are passive and stretched until the top of the backswing is reached. Then they actively contract to bring about a braking or retarding movement to stop the backswing. At this point, those muscles that had initiated the backswing diminish their active role and are involved only in a fixing or stabilizing capacity.

All the force that must be imparted to the clubhead is generated in the downswing. This is accomplished by having the clubhead arrive at the point of impact at its maximum speed, with the clubhead pointing in the required direction. The lateral hip movement plays a very critical role at this point and it is the factor that anyone who has mastered the secret of long driving has conquered. The downswing should begin with a forward movement of the hips. Cochran and Stobbs estimated that with most good golfers this takes place approximately "0.1 seconds before the clubhead reaches the limit of its backswing" (Ref. 2, p. 82). This forward

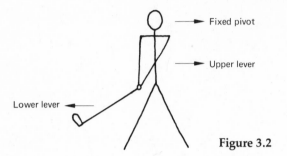

Fixed pivot

Upper lever

Lower lever

Figure 3.2

motion of the hips rotates the whole upper body and moves both levers in the "two-lever principle" referred to in the section on GRIP. The upper lever corresponds to the arms and shoulders swinging about the fixed pivot of the spine and head, and the lower lever is the club swinging about the wrists and hands, acting as a hinge. (See Fig. 3.2) Hay has stated that "this forward movement of the hips and the lesser forces exerted by the same hip and leg muscles later in the downswing have been estimated to account for 2½ of the total 3–4 hp generated in a good drive" (Ref. 8, p. 280). Cochran and Stobbs refer to the legs and hips as "the engine of the swing" and the arms and hands as "the transmission system" (Ref. 2, p. 81). There is no doubt that the hips and legs constitute an important source of power in long driving.

This system of two levers mentioned previously and referred to in Fig. 3.2, when swung around a fixed pivot in a single inclined plane

> will produce a more efficient application of energy than either of the single-lever systems. It is capable, in principle, of delivering into the clubhead at impact up to four-fifths of the total energy generated in the whole swing, and thus of making the clubhead travel almost twice as fast as could a fixed-spoke swing for the same total energy generated (Ref. 2, p. 11).

How this two-lever system actually works is a bit more complicated. In this system is a built-in *stop* which prevents the two levers from *jack-knifing* or opening out to more than about 90° in either direction. This stop is due to the golfer's inability to bend his wrists back more than 90° or so at the top of the backswing or at any other position as is explained in the section on grips and wrist action.

Let us start from a position at the top of the backswing where the lower lever (club) is hinged back at about 90° to the upper lever (arms and

Figure 3.3

shoulders). (See Fig. 3.3.) At the start of the downswing the lower lever follows the swing of the upper lever around the upper lever's fixed pivot (head and spine) and stays at a constant angle to it. In other words, the positions of the shoulders, arms, hands, and club relative to one another are unchanged as the hips are driven forward. Maintaining a constant angle between the club and the hands as long as possible will increase the force available to uncock or unleash the lower lever at the moment of impact. Very soon though, centrifugal force (a force involved in any movement about an axis and describing an arc which throws the object away from the center of the arc or hub, at a tangent to that arc) begins to throw the lower lever outwards so that it begins to catch up with the upper lever. Cochran and Stobbs further explain that:

> while this is happening, momentum is effectively being fed outwards from the upper lever to the lower lever, and most particularly to the extreme bottom end of it, which corresponds in an actual golfer to the clubhead. As a part of the reaction between the two levers, this process automatically slows down the swing of the upper lever, as it speeds up still further the swinging-out of the lower lever. (Ref. 2, p. 10)

In other words, when the left arm reaches a position approximately horizontal to the ground, this *one-piece* stage of the shoulders, arms, hands and club working as a single unit at the start of the downswing comes to an end and the angle between clubshaft and left arm becomes progressively larger. From this point on, the hands continue to move along their circular arc at a fairly constant speed while the clubhead's speed increases dramatically as the angle between the left arm and the clubshaft straightens out. It is a good example of a well-known law in physics—the Conservation of Angular Momentum—and displays the meaning behind the "delayed wrist snap," "whip," "releasing the angle," or "uncocking" phrases used so often in golf.

This brings us to the point of impact where the critical features of position of the clubhead and clubface and velocity at which the clubhead is moving play a crucial role. Since velocity or speed is so important at this stage, *follow-through* must also be considered. The principal power during the follow-through is the momentum in the clubhead itself and that explains its purpose. All the energy being generated to hit the ball should be at its maximum at impact. The clubhead should be accelerating as it makes contact with the ball so that its velocity will be at its greatest. The follow-through is essential to absorb this work and energy of the clubhead and body that led to the moment of impact. Without follow-through, the speed of the clubhead would have to diminish gradually prior to contact or stop abruptly at contact, thereby dissipating much of the available force.

Besides clubhead speed, the transfer of weight laterally or towards the target also contributes to force by putting the body weight into the stroke. Weight transfer moves the center of the arc slightly forward and thus flattens the vertical arc of the swing, keeping the clubhead low for a longer period and giving more time in the swing during which the clubhead can hit through the ball in the direction of the desired movement. For most efficient striking, the back of the left wrist at impact is pointed towards the target and fractionally ahead of the clubhead. Only if the ball is contacted squarely is all the force available imparted to the ball. Any hits off-center dissipate much of the generated force.

The degree to which the forces produced by the body are effective in moving the ball also depends upon the firmness of the grip and wrists at impact. Firmness of the wrists and grip prevents any recoil of the clubhead at the time of contact and makes the club an extension of the left arm so that upper and lower levers merge to form one long lever at impact, thereby generating more force and yielding greater distance. Without a firm connection at the hands, the lever length is shortened to stop at the hands or at the point of connection. The shorter lever, as mentioned previously, directly relates to less distance.

The counterpressure of the ground against the feet also affects the degree to which force produced by the body is transferred to the ball. Newton's Third Law of Action–Reaction states that for every action there is an equal and opposite reaction. Pressing downward and laterally with the legs and feet at impact results in a counterpressure exerted by the ground upwards and forward. Any slipping of the feet means a loss of force against the ball since some of the force is used in moving the foot or feet. Cleats on golf shoes offer a more secure base of support and help solve part of this problem, but stance also affects the friction available. If the feet are directly under the hips, the pressure of the feet is more directly downward and slipping is less likely to occur. When the feet are placed wider than hip-width apart, a more diagonal force is applied and the outward component of this force makes slipping more likely to occur.

Strokes for Accuracy

Putting, of course, falls into the category of a stroke demanding accuracy. However, the analysis of putting technique is included in the following section. This section deals primarily with the mechanics of the short approach shots, such as the pitch, pitch-and-run, or chip shots.

The direction of a ball's flight is dependent upon:

the direction in which the clubhead is moving at impact;
the angle of the face of the clubhead;
the relationship of the clubhead to the ball's center of gravity;
any outside forces acting on the ball (e.g., wind);
spin.

The angle of rebound is determined primarily by the angle of the clubface. This rebound angle is equal and opposite to the angle between the club and the ball. That is why a ball struck with a more lofted club (e.g., a 9-iron vs. a 3-iron) will rebound off the face of that club at a greater angle and with a higher trajectory. This angle of takeoff from the clubface will also equal the angle at which the ball will contact the green. Higher shots will drop more vertically on the green and will roll less because they have less of a horizontal component. Low shots will roll more because they lack the necessary vertical component and contact the green at a smaller angle.

The more nearly the clubface approximates a right angle to the desired path of the ball, the more accurately the ball will travel along its intended path. Having a straightforward path of the clubhead with the face perpendicular at impact is more easily accomplished if the clubhead follows a path along the desired line of flight both before and after impact. A square stance aids in keeping the swing along this track or path, but a square stance also allows for more body rotation backward at a time when control and accuracy are more important. Therefore, many authorities recommend the *open* stance to allow for more freedom of movement on the follow-through and to inhibit the amount of body rotation in order to keep the swing more vertical and along the desired path.

Again, if the grip is not firm at impact, the clubface will turn when the ball is contacted, making the direction the ball will travel unpredictable.

Repeating the principle that the angle of rebound is equal and opposite to the angle of incidence, we see that a ball struck with the clubface *open* will rebound to the right; one struck with a *closed* clubface will rebound to the left.

Some amount of spin is necessary to keep the ball on line after impact in order to counteract the air pressure built up whenever a golf ball moves through the air at a high velocity. The angle of any clubface is such that contact is first made below center of the ball, thereby resulting in backspin. Topspin is never achieved with any accurate hit in golf. Topspin only results when a ball is mis-hit above center, as when the ball is *topped*. At times it may be desirable to produce left or right spin on the ball, as on a dog-leg hole; but for the average golfer, right or left spin causes loss of strokes because it takes the ball well away from the straight line to the hole.

It is quite obvious how wind affects ball flight and accuracy. A wind blowing from right to left, for instance, will draw the ball left and therefore should be played more to the right to allow for the wind factor. In other words, shots should be aimed *into* the wind. How much the angle into the wind needs to be adjusted depends on the force of the wind.

Allowance must also be made for various contours of fairways and greens, keeping in mind that downhill slopes will cause the ball to roll farther and sidehill slopes will cause the ball to bounce or roll toward the lower side.

In the short approach shots, most of the attention is on accuracy and not distance. The adjustments for long distances on the approaches are therefore made in the length of the backswing, rather than in body rotation and lateral weight transfer. The two-lever system discussed in detail under *Strokes for Distance* still applies although the "rolling" of the left hand either to a *square* or *open* position at the top is de-emphasized. The angle of the upper lever in relation to the lower lever is lessened, since *hinging* or *cocking* is not encouraged because the extra force and energy generated by the wrist delay or *snap* is not essential when accuracy is being considered. Of utmost importance for these shots is control and accuracy of contact. Any unnecessary or extraneous movements detract from these two factors. For this reason, many people advocate more of a *one-piece* swing for shots demanding accuracy.

Putting

Unlike driving, where the need for maximum clubhead speed at impact largely determines the body actions that can be employed, success in putting can be achieved using a wide variety of techniques. There are as many putting styles as there are golfers and logically so because there are so few principles that must be followed in successful putting and so many ways in which these can be accomplished. Whether the golfer assumes a wide or a narrow stance is not important since the force needed is usually not great enough to require a transfer of weight. The main thing is that the golfer feel well-balanced.

Little light has been shed by research on which methods of putting (stroke or tap, hands together or apart, inverted hand position, etc.) are most suitable. The truth of this statement was borne out by results of a picture analysis of 16 top-rated professionals in which it was found that the only features where the professionals showed a measure of consistency were the ball position opposite the left foot and the head position with the eyes almost directly over the ball[2].

Cochran and Stobbs list three separate mechanical processes to be considered in putting:

(1) there's the whole business of getting the right part of the clubface to the ball moving in the right direction and at the right speed; (2) there's the actual impact between putter and ball; and (3) there's the roll of the ball across the green. (Ref. 2, p. 128)

The first process is only partly determined by mechanical considerations, most of which were explained in the section on *Strokes for Accuracy*. A great deal is *mental* or is affected by the psychological frame of mind of the golfer relating to optimism or pessimism in making certain putts.

The putter, having a vertical surface, contacts the ball just about at its center. Since the force is applied forward through the center of gravity, for all practical purposes, it is impossible to put any useful spin on the ball. Immediately after being struck with a putter, the ball at first does not role, but slides.[2] As it does so, friction between its cover and the grass begins at once to slow it down until the spin rate and the forward speed match and the ball starts to roll.

Since accuracy is a major problem in putting, it is important that the stroke be smooth and not jerky. This is why many golf instructors oppose "tap" methods of putting because, in this case, there is no follow-through and the swing must be cut by a muscular force opposing the forward movement. This jerking of the muscles not only makes it impossible to judge force imparted, but is likely to turn the face of the club from the perpendicular relationship to the line of the putt causing the ball to go off at an angle. A low backswing and follow-through along the line of putt insure a smoother stroke.

Putting has much in common with some of the mechanics of the short approach shots. The amount of force that will be imparted to the ball is regulated by changing the length of the swing. Judgment of surface and contour have to be considered. Keeping the clubface perpendicular to the line of putt also aids putting accuracy.

Cochran and Stobbs[2] found that the direction in which the ball travels is governed more by the direction in which the face of the putter is pointing than by the direction that the putter head is moving. Having the blade *square* at impact is therefore the most important single point to concentrate on in holing out. They also found that a comparison of the performances of professionals using blade, center-shafted, and mallet-style putters during tournament play revealed that no one type was significantly better than the others.

Some individuals have developed a *spot putting* technique, similar to the *spot bowling* technique used by many advanced bowlers. They simply sight a spot along the desired putting line relatively close to the ball. It is assumed that accuracy is improved because a close object or target is easier to hit than a far object. Also, the spot is within the line of vision so that sighting over the ball with its discrepancies in putting angle for long putts is not a factor in attempting judgment.

Any method for immobilizing parts of the body not needed for the stroke aids in accuracy because some of the chances for error are thus eliminated. Style is not important as long as it facilitates a smooth stroke that follows the line of the putt.

References

1. Broer, Marion. *Efficiency of Human Motion* (3rd edition). Philadelphia, Pa.: W. B. Saunders Co., 1973.
2. Cochran, Alastair and John Stobbs. *The Search for the Perfect Swing.* Philadelphia, Pa.: J. B. Lippincott Co., 1968.
3. Bunn, John W. *Scientific Principles of Coaching.* Englewood Cliffs, N.J.: Prentice-Hall, Inc., 1965.
4. Walker, Alan. *The Relationship of Distance and Accuracy to Three Golf Grips.* M.S. thesis, Springfield, Mass.: Springfield College, 1964.
5. Hicks, Betty. *Fundamentals of Golf.* Chicago, Ill.: J. A. Dubow Mfg. Co., 1948.
6. Jones, Ernest and Innis Brown. *Swinging into Golf.* New York, N.Y.: Robert M. McBride and Co., 1946.
7. Morrison, Alex J. *Better Golf without Practice.* New York, N.Y.: Simon & Schuster, 1940.
8. Hay, James G. *The Biomechanics of Sports Techniques.* Englewood Cliffs, N.J.: Prentice-Hall, Inc., 1973.

4
The Grip

Many lengthy papers have been written about the importance of various phases of the golf swing; namely, the stance, the grip, the balance, the timing and rhythm, the dominance of the left side, the size of the arc, and the stability of the head. Many arguments could rage if we were to try to select *the* single most important phase. It probably would be best to say that a good swing encompasses all of these, and one of the top priorities must be given the grip.

Your grip is the one link between you and your club face. If your grip is good, it helps your communication between your mind and the club face. You have a better chance to control the club face. You send all of your thoughts down through your arms, your telegraph lines, directly to your club face. Your grip is electrified by your thoughts.

When we dissect the hand action, it seems vital to understand the physical structure of the wrists and their role through the swinging action in order to better know the reasons, the whats and the whys, of what we are asked to do. Many times what feels natural to you, because of your hand action in another closely related sport, is not the simplest way to place your hands in the golf grip. A *comfortable* wrist action may not be the one that produces the best results throughout the golf swing.

In simple terms, the wrist has three basic moves that are made possible through the eight-bone structure of the wrist joint and the two bones of the lower arm. Try these three by holding the left hand straight out, thumb on top, back of the hand to the target

1. Move the hand in a forward and backward action, toward and away from the target, like the hinge on a door (Fig. 4.1a).
2. Move the hand up and down with the thumb moving toward and away from the nose (Fig. 4.1b).
3. Move the hand in a rotating motion with either the back or the palm of hand toward the sky (Fig. 4.1c).

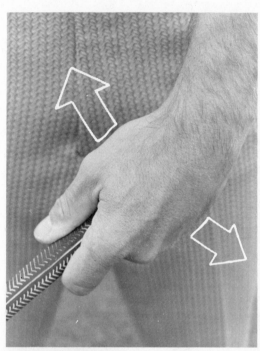

a) Door-hinge motion

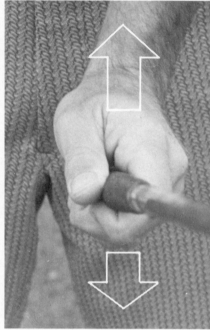

b) Hammering motion

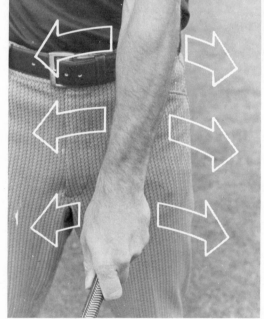

Fig. 4.1   Wrist motions

c) Rotating motion

In general, you have certain degrees of flexibility in these movements that are individual to you and therefore vary slightly in appearance. The aim is to establish the simplest basic movement with the wrists that accomplish the two major goals of a golf swing:

1. a straight or square-to-the-target club face at impact;
2. maximum club head speed at impact.

General

1. Praying hand position (Fig. 4.2): back of left hand to the target—palm of right hand to the target.
2. The grip should contribute to one unit movement—left and right hands working together as one.
3. The grip should bring the club face square to the ball at impact.
4. The hands should transmit power from the motion of the body to the club head.

Fig. 4.2 Praying hands position: Back of left hand toward target, palm of right hand toward target

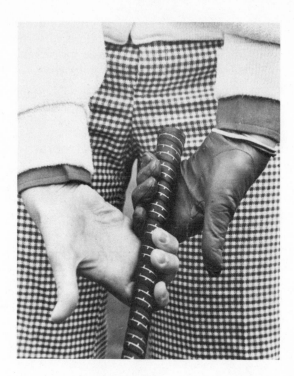

Fig. 4.3 Pressure points—opposing forces—pressure on sides of the club

5. The back of the left hand and the face of the club should both be aligned to the target at address position.
6. If you feel the pressure of the fingers along the sides of the club (see Fig. 4.3) the club face at impact will have a better chance of remaining square; otherwise, when the ball and club meet at impact, the face may open up.
7. Grip should be firm, alive; but never taut or deathlike. Try not to strangle the club.

Variations of the Grip

The three grips are almost the same—only the position of the little finger changes.

1. *The Ten Finger Grip* is good for small hands, especially for those of juniors and women, because all ten fingers are on the club (Fig. 4.4), which gives you more finger contact on club for added feel and strength.

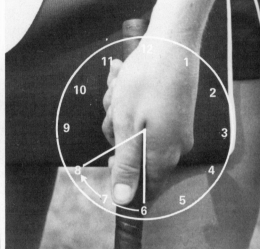

◀ **Fig. 4.4** Full- or ten-finger grip (bottom view)

Fig. 4.5 Left-hand grip

◀ **Fig. 4.6** Pressure on last three fingers of left hand

A. *Left Hand*

    i) The back of the left hand faces the target. (See Fig. 4.5.)

    ii) The club is placed diagonally across the left palm.

    iii) The thumb is placed on the club from 6:00 to 8:00 position; try not to overextend thumb down shaft or draw it up excessively.

    iv) As you look down at the back of the hand, one to two knuckles should show. (Refer to the clock in Fig. 4.5 for knuckle position.)

    v) The "V" formed by the index finger and the thumb points to the right of center.

    vi) Grip the club firmly with the last three fingers. (See Fig. 4.6.)

B. *Right Hand (Fig. 4.7)*

    i) The right palm faces the target.

    ii) The groove or lifeline covers the left thumb.

    iii) The club is held in the fingers of the right hand.

    iv) The thumb is on the club at 5:00 and normal extension, thumb presses club into index finger (simulates trigger finger).

    v) As you look down, you should see the index finger knuckle and possibly the middle finger knuckle.

    vi) The "V" formed by the index finger and the thumb points to the nose or slightly to the right of center.

    vii) Feel pressure on the side of the club with middle three fingers.

2. *Interlocking Grip.* This grip gives the feeling of compactness between the two hands, because the index finger of the left and little finger of the right interlock (Fig. 4.8). Caution should be used to prevent too much pressure between interlocking fingers, as this has a tendency to over-pressurize the grip and force the palms upward.

A. *Left Hand*

    i) The back of left hand faces the target. (See Fig. 4.5.)

    ii) The club is placed diagonally across the left palm.

    iii) The thumb is placed on the club from 6:00 to 8:00 position; try to neither over-extend thumb down shaft nor draw it up excessively.

    iv) As you look down at the back of the hand, one to two knuckles should show. (Refer to the clock in Fig. 4.5 for knuckle position.)

    v) The "V" formed by the index finger and the thumb points to the right of center.

    vi) Grip the club firmly with the last three fingers.

B. *Right Hand*

    i) The right palm faces the target.

    ii) The groove, or life line, covers the left thumb.

    iii) The club is held in the fingers of the right hand.

    iv) The thumb is on the club at 5:00 and normal extension, thumb presses club into index finger (simulates trigger finger) as shown in Fig. 4.9.

    v) As you look down, you should see the index finger knuckle and possibly the middle finger knuckle.

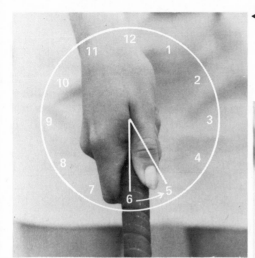

◀Fig. 4.7 Right-hand grip

▲
Fig. 4.8 Interlocking grip (bottom view)

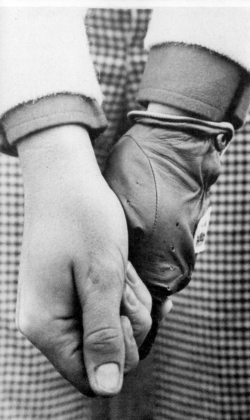

Fig. 4.9 Front view at address

vi) The "V" formed by the index finger and the thumb points to the nose or slightly to the right of center.

vii) Interlock small finger of the right hand with the index finger of the left. (See Fig. 4.8.)

3. *Overlapping Grip.* This is the most popular grip as it allows more flexibility for hand structures when placing the hands on the club properly (Fig. 4.10).

A. *Left Hand*

i) The back of left hand faces the target. (See Fig. 4.5 above.)

ii) The club is placed diagonally across the left palm.

iii) The thumb is placed on the club from 6:00 to 8:00 position; try not to over-extend thumb down shaft or draw it up excessively.

iv) As you look down at the back of the hand, one to two knuckles should show. (Refer to the clock in Fig. 4.5 for knuckle position.)

Fig. 4.10 Vardon or overlapping grip (bottom view)

v) The "V" formed by the index finger and the thumb points to the right of center.

vi) Grip firmly with the last three fingers.

B. *Right Hand*

   i) The right palm faces the target.

   ii) The groove or life line covers the left thumb.

   iii) The club is held in the fingers of the right hand.

   iv) The thumb is on the club at 5:00 and normal extension, thumb presses club into index finger (simulates trigger finger). (See Fig. 4.7.)

   v) As you look down, you should see the index finger knuckle and possible the middle finger knuckle.

   vi) The "V" formed by the index finger and the thumb points to the nose or slightly to the right of center.

   vii) The little finger of the right hand overlaps the side of the index finger of the left hand; it does not hang on, dig in, or hook the index finger but allows the hands to move closer together so that they can work as one unit.

Common Errors	Corrections
Left Hand	
1. Hand rotated too far to the right, so that the left wrist has a tendency to lock at impact; three or four knuckles show; this results in a hook from excessive rotation of lower arm and hands or in a dramatic slice when the hand is frozen open at impact (Fig. 4.11).	Check to see that only one or two knuckles show on the back of the left hand. This allows the normal action of the left wrist at impact.

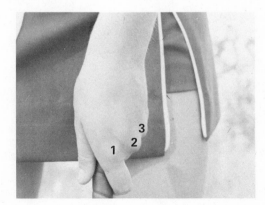

Fig. 4.11 Excessive rotation to right

Common Errors	**Corrections**
2. Thumb placed off of the grip of the club and resting on fingers of left hand (Fig. 4.12).	Place thumb at 6:00 to 8:00. Check to see that thumb is under the shaft at the top of the back swing.
3. Relaxing finger pressure in last three fingers of left hand at the top of the back swing (Fig. 4.13).	Maintain firm grip with the last three fingers of the left hand, at top and through entire swing.
4. Thumb extended too far down shaft or drawn up excessively (Figs. 4.14 to 4.20).	Draw up or extend to normal length, which places the tip of thumb on a line even with the bent index finger.
5. Left hand rotated too far to left (Fig. 4.21).	Check to see that only one or two knuckles show on the back of the left hand.

Figure 4.12

Figure 4.13

◀**Fig. 4.14**   Long thumb—right hand

Fig. 4.15   Long thumbs—front view

Fig. 4.16   Long thumbs—side view

Fig. 4.17   Short thumb—left ▶ hand

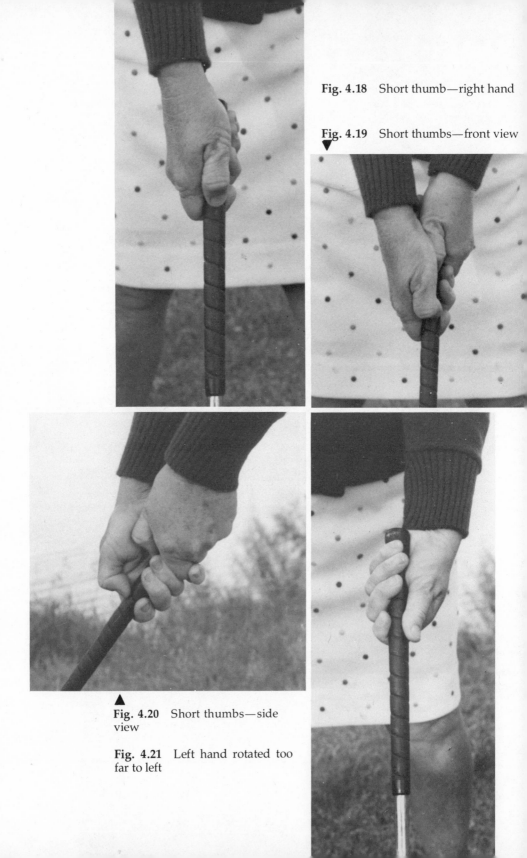

Fig. 4.18 Short thumb—right hand

Fig. 4.19 Short thumbs—front view

Fig. 4.20 Short thumbs—side view

Fig. 4.21 Left hand rotated too far to left

Common Errors

Corrections

Right Hand

1. Hand rotated too far to the right (Fig. 4.22); so that the right wrist has a tendency to lock at impact; this forces either extreme counterclockwise rotation or frozen-open club face at impact. The extreme rotation produces a hook; the locking action a dramatic slice.

   Feel the club in the fingers with palm facing target; make sure "V" is on top, almost pointing to the nose. (See Fig. 4.7.)

2. Right hand rotated too far left (Fig. 4.23); this helps set up a dominant right side which forces you to swing up and over the ball at impact.

   Palm facing target, see index finger knuckle. (See Fig. 4.7.)

3. Thumb to the right of center, bracing against side of shaft away from target.

   Place thumb at 5:00. (See Fig. 4.7.)

4. Squeezing little finger too tightly over index, or in interlocking, too tightly with index.

   Allow little finger to relax enough to maintain firm grip, but not enough to inhibit togetherness feeling in hands.

◀**Fig. 4.22** Right hand rotated too far to right

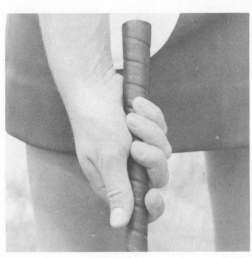

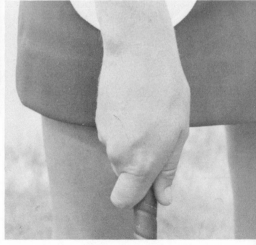

Fig. 4.23 Right hand rotated too far to left ▶

Common Errors

Corrections

Both Hands

1. Allowing the hands to separate on the club grip so there is a space between the left and right hands.

   Make sure that lifeline of right hand covers the thumb of the left hand; maintain a one unit feeling. (See Fig. 4.9.)

2. Rotating both hands to the right of the shaft, with back of left hand to sky and palm of right to the sky (Fig. 4.24).

   Check alignment—back of the left hand to the target, palm of the right hand to the target. (See Fig. 4.2.)

3. Picking up club with a cocking wrist action at start of the take-away.

   Take the club low to ground for first 6″ to 12″ away from ball. (See Fig. 4.25.)

Fig. 4.24 Both hands rotated to right of shaft

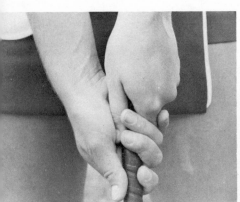

Fig. 4.25 Correction for cocking wrist action

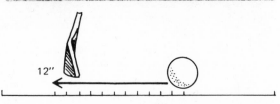

Take club low to ground for first 6″ to 12″ away from ball.

Practice Suggestions

1. Squeeze a ball or spring exerciser in the left hand to gain grip strength. Try using just the last three fingers.
2. Put hands together in a praying position in front of you, lower them to address position, and practice a take-away and follow through. (See Figs. 4.26, 4.27, and 4.28.)

Fig. 4.26 Practice praying hands position—address

Fig. 4.27 Take-away—backswing

Fig. 4.28 Follow through

3. Swing a weighted club or *swing-right* bar to strengthen the hands and the arms.

4. Carry books or packages with the left hand and arm.

5. Put an "X" on the back of your left hand close to knuckles "3" and "4." Place hand on the club. Swing to the top of the swing with a firm wrist without being able to see the "X" at any time during your normal back swing.

6. Practice hitting short and full shots with just your left hand swinging the club (Fig. 4.29).

7. Take the club in the fingers of the right hand and tap the ground as if you were hammering a nail into a board. Repeat with both hands on the club. This is a check to see if grip is correct. You will feel hammering action with the proper grip.

8. Take the club in the last three fingers of left hand and twirl counterclockwise.

9. Take club in last three fingers of right hand and twirl counterclockwise. This strengthens your fingers and the muscles of your forearms and develops them for increased effectiveness of the pressure on the sides of the club at impact.

10. Extend left arm as if holding golf club in left hand. Place sheet of newspaper in hand and wad up until whole sheet is in shape of small ball. Repeat with right hand.

11. Place hands very gently on club. Take normal back swing and notice how pressure instinctively increases as you start your forward swing.

Fig. 4.29 Practice using left hand only

5
Stance

Your stance is your foundation. Just as a good building has a sound foundation, so must your golf swing be built on a strong foundation. You establish your alignment through the placement of your feet. With your feet and spikes you dig into the surface; you get ready to go; you wiggle-waggle; you feel the tension build; you find your balance; you find the sameness of approach to the ball each time.

From the waist down you feel down to the ball—a downward and inward feeling with the resistance on the inner parts of the feet. As Newton's law states, "for every force there is a resisting force." In a golf swing the resisting force in the lower part of the body activates the upper part of the body so that you can swing harder and faster.

Alignment

Position entire body and club head in alignment with target at address position (Fig. 5.1).

1. *Club Alignment*

   A. Place club face directly behind ball, square to target line.

   B. From the position shown in Fig. 5.1, using the scoring lines and the sole line, draw a line perpendicular to the target line and extend it toward you (Fig. 5.2).

   C. Take your stance to the proper width on either side of this line perpendicular to the target line; e.g., full swing—place feet together. (Refer to position 1 in Fig. 5.3.) Take a 6- to 10-inch step toward target with left foot. (Refer to position 2 in Fig. 5.3.) Take an 8- to 12-inch step away from target with right foot. (Refer to position 3 in Fig. 5.3.)

Fig. 5.1 Club face directly behind ball—square to target line

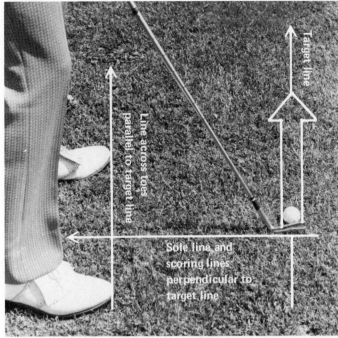

Target line

Line across toes
parallel to target line

Sole line and
scoring lines
perpendicular to
target line

Fig. 5.2 Club
alignment

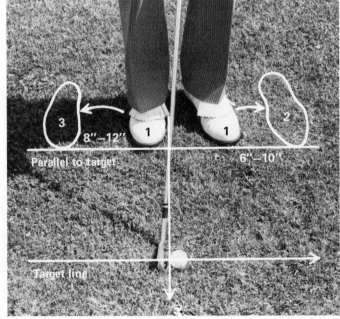

3

8"–12"

Parallel to target

1   1

2

6"–10"

Target line

1. Feet together.
2. Left foot steps
   toward target
   6–10 inches.
3. Right foot steps
   away from target
   8–12 inches.

Fig. 5.3 Aligning
feet

2. *Body Alignment* (Fig. 5.4)

    A. Take a square stance—toes on a line parallel to target line;

    B. Align your hips and shoulders on a line parallel to the target line.

Square Stance

Square stance is used for most of the shots in golf.

1. Place your feet about as far apart as the width of your shoulders.

2. The toes of your shoes should be in a line parallel to the line of flight.

3. You may rotate your left foot slightly out toward the target (Fig. 5.5).

Fig. 5.4 Body alignment square to target line

Fig. 5.5 Square stance, left foot slightly out

4. Your right foot remains perpendicular to the line of flight.

5. You may square your stance with your heels. That way you can rotate the toes of either foot or both feet out and still be in a square stance.

6. Flex your knees slightly, like a basketball player getting ready to make a free throw, or a player ready to receive a tennis serve (Fig. 5.6).

7. Bend from the hips, *rear* out, as if someone hit you in the abdomen, or like a football player in a blocking position (Fig. 5.7).

8. Let your arms hang down at sides. They should hang in front of hips. If they hang against the outside of legs, push your seat further out.

9. Your weight should be equally distributed on each foot. Feel the pressure on the inside borders of the feet.

Fig. 5.6 Upright position too straight —arms hang at side of hips

Fig. 5.7 Rear out, bend from hips— arms should hang in front of hips

Open Stance

An open stance (Figs. 5.8 and 5.9) is used to create a slice or pull, produce a cutting action on the ball for short shots or for shots to produce more height and backspin. It can also be used for sand shots. Shoulders, hips and knees are aligned to the left of the target.

1. Move your left foot slightly back from the line of flight.
2. Turn your left toe slightly out.

Fig. 5.8   Open stance—side view

Fig. 5.9   Open stance—front view
▼

Closed Stance

A closed stance (Figs. 5.10 and 5.11) is used to create a hook or push. It is used for short chip shots. Shoulders, hips, and knees are lined up to the right of the target.

1. Move your right foot back from the line of the flight.
2. Your body should be slightly closed to the line of the flight.

Fig. 5.10   Closed stance—side view
▼

Fig. 5.11   Closed stance—front view ▶

Full Swing

1. *Irons*

   A. Keep your stance as wide as the width of your shoulders;

   B. Place the ball from centered to a little left of center. Placement depends upon the skill of the player—a beginner will have better results hitting from the center of the stance while a more advanced golfer will move the ball closer to the left foot;

2. *Woods* (Fig. 5.12)

   A. *Driver.* Play the ball inside the heel of the left foot because the ball is elevated on the tee and is hit more on the upswing;

   B. *Fairway woods.* Play the ball toward the left foot; keep the club head low to the ground through the hitting zone (see uneven lies for other foot positions).

Short Swing

1. Narrow your stance, because your feet should be closer together than they are for a full swing (Fig 5. 13). The feeling of littleness starts in your feet.

2. Use a slightly open stance with your left foot slightly open to the target line.

3. Flex your knees; lower your center of gravity to get a feeling of being down over the ball—you feel stable over the ball.

4. Place the ball in the center to slightly left of center.

Putting

1. Your stance may be varied. You may have a narrow stance or a wide stance.

2. Either distribute your weight equally on each foot or shift it so that most of the weight is on the left foot.

3. Your stance may be square, open, or closed, whichever feels more comfortable for you.

4. Play the ball anywhere you wish. Usually it is played from the center of your stance to off of your left toe (Fig. 5.14).

Fig. 5.12 Using woods

Fig. 5.13 Short swing
▼

Fig. 5.14 Putting

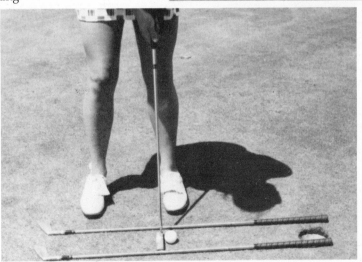

Common Errors	Corrections
1. If your stance is too wide in your full swing, you will have a planted type of stance which will restrict your pivot.	Your stance should be about the width of your shoulders.
2. Your weight is more on your right foot at address.	Your weight should be equally distributed on both feet, feeling pressure on inner borders of your feet.
3. Your weight is more on your left foot at address during full swing.	Your weight should be equally distributed on both feet.
4. Hooked ball	Check to see if your stance is too closed and try to square your feet.
5. Sliced ball	Check to see if your stance is too open and try to square your feet. Hit inside and out on target line.

Practice Suggestions

1. You may use clubs to help you get the proper alignment. Lay one club on the ground for your foot line and another club parallel to it for the target line. Add a third club perpendicularly across the two clubs for the ball placement line forming a figure H, as shown in Fig. 5.15.

2. Practice using a square stance to help you hit a straight ball that is aligned well to the target line.

3. Practice using a closed stance to see what kind of a shot you get.

4. Practice using an open stance to see what kind of a shot you get.

5. Have your partner check your alignment.

Fig. 5.15 Alignment exercise

6
Distance—or Full—Swing

The purpose of the golf swing is to bring the club head squarely along the intended line to the target through the impact area at maximum speed. In learning the full swing, you must concentrate on the feeling of power and distance. You swing the arms, then coil or turn your upper body, so that it allows you to get your hands and arms higher. The lower body then moves toward the target pulling the arms and hands after it. This pulling force of the hands and body along with the delayed club head produces centrifugal force, increasing the club head speed at impact. The right side of your swing is your enemy—it is *only* a supporting member of the cast. The left side is your friend—it is always the dominant leader.

Full Swing (General)

The full swing is taking the club to the top of your back swing and with a pulling action returning the club squarely to the ball with maximum speed and then continuing on to a high finish.

Back swing

1. *Club selection*

    A. Pick the club that will produce the shot you want to make.

2. *Grip*—Take your choice between:

    A. full ten finger grip,

    B. interlocking grip,

    C. overlapping grip.

3. *Alignment*

    A. From behind the ball, sight down the line to the target.

    B. Place the club square to the line to the target.

4. *Stance*

    A. Use a square stance, about the width of your shoulders;

    B. Distribute your weight equally on both feet so that you have a feeling of pressure on the inner borders of the feet.

    C. Have a wiggle-waggle or a forward press.

5. *Address position*

    A. Placing your feet together on a line perpendicular to the target, take a step with the left foot, 6″ to 10″ towards the target; take your big step with the right foot about 8″ to 12″ away from the target. Keep your left shoulder slightly higher than the right shoulder;

    B. Set your left side up in a strong position with your left arm and club as one;

    C. The right side of your body is submissive—right arm relaxed;

    D. Your knees are slightly flexed; bend from hips, rear out—watch not to tuck your seat under or do a deep knee bend;

    E. Using the triangle formation in your arms to form the "V" or "Y," extend arms out from your body, bend from your hips and lower your chin (Fig. 6.1).

6. *Back Swing-execution*

    A. Start the swing in one piece; hands, arms, shoulders, hips should be together. The hands have the longest way to go, so they may initiate the back swing.

    B. Take the club straight back on the target line 6″ to 12″.

    C. Take the club back in the triangular motion to between knee high and waist high. Then your right elbow will hinge bend. Continue upward until your hands are about shoulder height or a little bit higher;

    D. Your left arm is firm; your right arm is hinged with the elbow pointing down.

    E. The club should not be more than parallel to the ground at the top of the back swing.

    F. At the top of the swing, your back should face the target (Fig. 6.2).

    G. Your left side will turn in slightly towards center.

    H. Your left knee will turn slightly toward center and the ball.

    I. Keep your head steady—do not sway.

    J. Your left heel may lift slightly off ground.

Fig. 6.1 Your arms form a V or a Y

Fig. 6.2 At top of swing your back ▶
is to target

K. Feel the weight on the inward part of your right foot build resistance.

L. Bend your right knee slightly—aim it straight out.

M. With your back facing the target, feel like stretching your muscles.

N. Pause—then start the down (forward) swing.

Forward Swing:

1. Start your forward swing with a pulling action of the lower left side.

2. Knees, hips, shoulders, arms-hands lead the forward swing, in that order.

3. Your weight shifts toward the left target side of body. (Figs. 6.3 and 6.4)

4. With slight inside motion, your right elbow comes in towards your body, and the plane of swing is slightly inside.

5. Keep your left arm firm—start with pulling action.

6. Delay your hitting action until your hands approach the ball—then release the blow. Club head will catch up just after impact and pass your hands.

7. Keep your head steady.

8. Your right shoulder should have a feeling of swinging under your chin.

9. Your right heel comes off the ground.

Figure 6.3

Figure 6.4

10. With good extension through the hitting area, hit through the ball, not to it.

11. Hit past your chin—get a feeling of sending the club head toward the target.

12. Have a feeling of letting your muscles unwind and spring forward.

13. Resist the temptation to spin on the ball (round-housing).

14. Keep the club head low and square through the hitting area.

15. Feel as if you are hitting straight along the target line.

16. After impact, finish high, towards the sky!

17. Your left arm is hinged and your right arm is firm.

18. Your abdomen, belt buckle, and knees are all facing towards the target when you finish the shot (Fig. 6.5).

Fig. 6.5 At completion of shot you should be facing target

Common Errors

Corrections

1. Swaying off of the ball on back swing.

During pivot and turn, your belt buckle should face slightly right of center with your back to the target. Make a good shoulder turn.

2. Picking up the club on the back swing.

Clip the grass as you take the club back. Reach the club back as if you want to hand the club to someone. Stretch. Take the club back as one piece. Keep the club low to the ground for the first 6" to 12". See Fig. 6.8.

3. Loss of balance from too narrow a stance.

Stance should be about the width of your shoulders. Have a downward and inward feeling in your feet.

4. Loss of balance on heels or on toes.

Emphasize weight on inner borders of feet with the weight toward the heel. Test by tapping heels and toes at address.

5. Hitting from the top of the back swing—a thrower—a slice or pull usually results.

Swing to the top of your back swing and stop. Then start the club down with a pulling motion of the lower left side; left arm pulls and right elbow comes close to your right side.

6. Swinging too far back at top of back swing.

a) Swing to the top of your swing and stop. Then look to see how high your hands are. The club should not be more than parallel to the ground. Feel like you are only taking a ¾-swing.

b) Tighten last three fingers on left hand.

c) Do not fan hands quickly on start of back swing.

7. Swinging the club on a flat plane.

Swing in a more upright plane—think ferris wheel, not merry-go-round.

8. Tucking rear under at address position.

Keep your rear-end out like someone poked you in the abdomen. Bend from the hips. Let your arms hang down in front of your hipline.

9. Rotating or fanning both hands to right at start of take-away. A hook often results.

Work for one unit take-away with little or no wrist action and no rotation of club face. Envision the club face as a ferris wheel seat which rotates without dumping the passengers out of their seats.

10. Hitting from inside to out on the target line, producing a pushed shot.

Keep the club on the target line at impact. Use tees on club path to see where path goes.

Practice Suggestions

1. Place thin blocks of wood under the outside of each foot so that you can feel the insides of your feet. This will help you to avoid swaying your whole body and to feel the inward parts of your feet.

2. Use your shadow to watch for upper body swaying, put a ball on your (shadow's) head (Fig. 6.6), and then swing, watching the ball to see if your (shadow's) head is moving off the ball (Fig. 6.7).

Fig. 6.6 Place ball on your (shadow's) head

Fig. 6.7 During swing, do not allow your (shadow's) head to move off ball

3. When picking up the club, put a tee about six inches in front of the ball and one about six inches behind the ball (Fig. 6.8). When you take the club back, try to hit the tee behind and on the follow-through try to hit the tee in front of the ball. This keeps the club head low through the hitting area.

4. Place your feet together (heels together) and swing the club back and forth; this will help with your balance.

5. Use a partner and have him step in behind you after you have taken a full back swing. Then have him place his hand on the club and resist the club as you start the down swing. This will give you a feeling of pulling the club.

6. Have your partner swing to the finish and have him pose and hold it as if someone was coming out to take his picture. This will give him the feeling of swinging to the finish.

7. Accelerate through the ball; hit past your chin; watch the ball and club meet. Turn the name of the ball so that you can read it; then try to read it at impact. This will help keep your head down through the hitting area.

8. Work on the timing of your golf swing. Slow back and accelerate through. Count one and two, swing back and through, swish the air, count as you swing. Sing songs like "Hello, Dolly." Just as in driving a car, finish your reverse motion before you shift gears to go forward.

9. Use the illustration of the "C" and "I" position. At the address position, you are bent into an imaginary "C" position and stay that way until you have hit the ball, and then you can turn out and become an imaginary "I" position.

10. Check sequence of swing. Hands are No. 1, arms No. 2, and hips No. 3. No. 1 starts back swing followed closely by 2 and 3. Hips (No. 3) start forward swing, followed by 2 and 1. Swing sequence 1-2-3, 3-2-1.

11. Towel exercise—hold twisted towel between your hands across at waist height, left hand palm down, right hand palm up. Keep towel stretched taut. Reach back, turning shoulders until back faces target. Start swing back towards target with left side. Finish in high follow-through, with belt buckle toward target. Repeat. After several times, swing to top of back swing and as you start forward, let go of towel with right hand. Pull towel with left hand only to a high finish.

12. Visualize a stripe around the center of a practice ball. Imagine that the ball is the world and the stripe is the equator (Fig. 6.9). When you hit the ball, always try to hit it below the equator in South America, or better yet, one-half inch below the South Pole. Any contact above the equator will cause a shot to have a low trajectory or even roll along the ground. Contact should always be made below the equator. The ideal

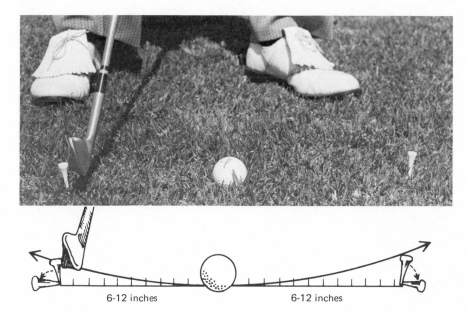

6-12 inches   6-12 inches

Figure 6.8

Figure 6.9

contact is from South America to ½ an inch *below* the South Pole when the sole takes a divot. The sole contacts the ground ½" below the ball. The ball contacts the middle of the club face.

13. Stand facing a friend who is in address position without a club. Reach out and hold his head gently on either side. With his hands separated, have him swing a normal back-to-target, belt-buckle-to-target swing. Repeat, having partner hold your head. Then, do the same exercise only holding hands about one inch from either side of head. Repeat.

14. *Club Exercise (in front).* Hold club across in front of you with the grip to the left and the club head to the right. Place your left hand palm down on grip end of club and your right hand palm up on right end of club. Take address position and swing club back and forth slowly, increasing the size of your swing. Work up to a full swing, then let the right hand slide down to meet the left hand and form the golf grip. Keep swinging back and forth.

Figure 6.10

Figure 6.11

15. *Club Exercise (behind back).* Place a club behind your back, across your waist. Loop your arms over the club on the right and left sides until you have the club in the crook of each elbow (Fig. 6.10). In the address position, make an imaginary swing, pointing at a ball on the ground with the left end of the club as you swing back, and the right end as you swing forward (Fig. 6.11).

16. Place club in left hand. Hit ten shots with left hand only. Now add *just the little finger* of the right hand in normal position. Three fingers and thumb are off the club, above the grip. Hit ten shots. Add ring finger of right hand in normal position. Two fingers and thumb are above and off the grip. Hit ten shots. Continue adding one finger at a time until completely normal grip is established for right hand. (Left hand will feel more dominant in this motion and drill.)

7
Short Shot

In teaching the full swing, we go to great lengths to give you the feeling of the power and distance required. Generally, we create and encourage a feeling of bigness and fullness of action. For the short shot, we now go to the same lengths to give you the feeling of control—directional thoughts. We will now form ideas that will make your control feel guided, measured, and projected toward a very specific target—the pin. How often, on television, we watch Arnold Palmer or Jack Nicklaus hit a booming drive with a mighty force behind it, only to watch seconds later while these great players literally hover in a most delicate, precise, and gentle manner over a short shot. This complete change of mood and action is what you should capture in your short shots.

General

1. *Description.* The short shot is used to get the ball onto the green from any distance starting from just off the green to as much as 75 yards away. When hitting the short shot, think of yourself as standing in front of a large clock (Fig. 7.1). The clock is behind you, your head is at 12:00, and your ball is at 6:00. To help measure distance in your short shot, take the club back to 7:00 and follow through to 5:00, or from 8:00 to 4:00, or from 9:00 to 3:00. The 7:00 to 5:00 swing produces a shot approximately 15 to 25 yards. The 8:00 to 4:00 swing produces a shot approximately 30 to 50 yards. The 9:00 to 3:00 swing produces a shot approximately 50 to 75 yards. The variations in these estimates depend on the individual's clubhead speed at impact.

2. *Execution*

   A. Use your standard grip and move your hands down on the club grip—choke it.

Fig. 7.1   Short shot—body position

Fig. 7.2   Short shot—side view

Fig. 7.3 Hands and arms swing as one unit away and toward target

B. Narrow your stance for close short shots—widen it a little for 50- to 75-yard shots (Fig. 7.2).

C. Use an open stance—place the ball center to left of center.

D. Lower your center of gravity; feel getting down to the shot.

E. Your weight should remain forward on your left foot for the 7:00 to 5:00 shot, but should be more equally distributed in the others. In the 8:00 to 4:00 and the 9:00 to 3:00 shots, there is a normal shift of weight during the shot.

F. Form a triangle with your arms and shoulders moving in a pendular action, swinging back from target and toward the target (Fig. 7.3).

G. Keep the club low to the ground; use a brushing and sweeping action.

H. The back of your left hand should face the target throughout the swing. Your left hand leads the forward swing and is never passed by the right hand. The club face is square to the target throughout the shot.

I. Use little or no wrist action throughout the swing.

J. Work for consistency in speed of hit and swing.

K. Vary the length of back swing and forward swing—never above the waist on either side; think little; keep swing between 9:00 and 3:00 (Fig. 7.4).

Fig. 7.4 Short shot sequence

L. Good players who are scoring well will get about 50 percent of these shots close enough for one putt.

M. Use the lower-numbered club when there is no need for height.

N. When choosing a club, consider the lie of the ball before you think about the distance needed.

Variations

Pitch and run

1. *Description.* Ball has low trajectory. Ball is hit in the air one-third of the total distance and rolls two-thirds. This is usually used close to the edge of the green (Fig. 7.5). Use a less-lofted club, usually 8-iron through 3-iron.

2. *Execution*

A. Place your hands farther down on grip of club—choke down.

B. Narrow your stance, with your left toe drawn back slightly —slightly open stance.

C. Flex your knees. You should have a sitting-down feeling.

D. Play the ball center to left of center.

E. Your club face should remain square throughout the swing, keeping the club low through the hitting area.

F. Keep your hands and arms close to the body.

G. Keep the stroke short and firm.

H. Swing the club straight away and straight toward the target.

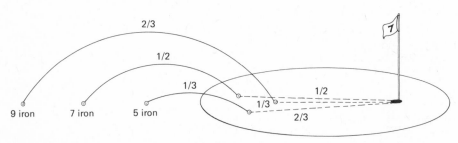

Fig. 7.5 Short shot diagram

Stop or lob shot

1. *Description.* The ball is hit high into the air with a soft, floating, gentle-chopping action. Use a more-lofted club, such as a 9-iron, pitching wedge, or sand wedge.

2. *Execution*

   A. Use your grip, stance, and body position as in the basic shot.

   B. Slow the speed of the swing down—change the tempo, swinging slower. If using a wedge, you will find that the club is heavier so it must be swung slower and back higher than normal—about 11:00 to 1:00.

   C. The club face should be square to slightly open to the line to the target.

   D. Use this shot when standard shot will not stop the ball.

   E. Your wrists may be more flexible on the back swing during this shot; make sure to have a higher back swing and follow through as if you were hitting over a high fence or hedge.

Cut shot—high trajectory

1. *Description.* This shot has a very high loft to it. The ball doesn't carry very far and has a very quick stopping action. Use a pitching wedge or sand wedge.

2. *Execution*

   A. Use your standard grip.

   B. Use an open stance.

   C. Be sure the club face is open at address and impact.

   D. There is more wrist action during this shot, allowing the club face to cut across the target line from outside to inside.

   E. Swing the club back farther than a normal swing for this distance; the tempo should be slower.

   F. Continuing on the outside-in pattern of this shot, finish by drawing your hand in across your body on the follow-through.

Half-shot

1. *Description.* There is a grey zone for most golfers that does not fit into the full shot description. This is called the half-shot. It is used at a time when you are hitting onto a green over the distance that you would normally hit a short shot, but when the accuracy of the short pendular motion is still required. You, then, need the pulling action

of the full shot and the firm pendular action of the short shot. If you call the full shot the pivot and the short shot the pendular then the combination shot is the "pivendular" shot.

2. *Execution*

A. Use your standard grip closer to the top of the grip of the club.

B. A square stance should be used.

C. Place the ball in the center of your stance.

D. Your back swing is to slightly above waist—about 10:00 position.

E. Use the pulling action of your body to *start* the forward swing.

F. There is little or no wrist action in this shot; it is a very pendular action with your hands and arms.

G. As the swing goes towards target, the follow-through is abbreviated, finishing with the hand at 2:00. The club face should be square to the target throughout the shot.

Common Errors   Corrections

Common Errors	Corrections
1. Gripping high on the club.	Grip club down farther on shaft; choke down.
2. Stance is too wide.	Narrow your stance to between 2 and 8 inches.
3. Weight is back on your right foot.	Have your weight equally distributed or have more weight on your left foot.
4. Allowing yourself to sway off the ball.	Use little or no body action in the shot.
5. Picking your club up too fast on the back swing.	Keep the club low to the ground throughout the swing.
6. Using loose and sloppy wrist action.	Use a pendular wrist, arm, and shoulder movement—firm wrist action (little or no wrist movement).
7. Your posture is too upright and tall.	Flex and bend knees—lower your center of gravity. Bend from the hips.
8. You are taking too high a back swing.	Swing your club no higher than 9:00 to 3:00, or waist to waist.
9. You hit the top half of the ball.	Brush the surface under ball, taking a divot and bruising the ground.
10. You vary the tempo of your swing inconsistently.	Work for a more consistent tempo of your swing for the majority of your short shots.
11. Hitting without mental picture of where the ball should land.	Hit for a dime or for a spot that you have chosen on the green.
12. Thinking of how you are going to miss the shot.	Think positively where the shot *should* go.

Practice Suggestions

1. Place your feet two inches apart on a line square or open to the target line. Weight is more toward the left foot. With a sit-down posture, flex the knees—get a feeling of "littleness." Make a triangle out of the arms and shoulders. Move arms away and toward the target making motion over the club on the ground. Add the club, gripping it well down on the leather grip; then with the club brush the ground ten times. After small divots have been taken, make same swing using the ball. Repeat with the 5-, 6-, 7-, 8-, 9-irons, and wedge. Learn the carry and roll of each club. Keep the tempo consistent. Practice your clock positions—7:00 to 5:00, 8:00 to 4:00, and 9:00 to 3:00.

2. Repeat hitting practices as above, using the 8-iron, 9-iron, and wedge, but this time vary the tempo, which causes the ball to stop sooner and creates the "soft" shot.

3. Place two clubs about six inches apart on either side of the target line (Fig. 7.6). Chip and pitch shots—the path of the swing is within the clubs. Narrow the distance to five inches and continue practice. Continue to narrow distance between clubs until shot can be made from the narrowest width.

Fig. 7.6 Track to target—practice between clubs for projection to target

4. Place three clubs on the green in a triangle. Chip shots into the triangle for spot practice. Continue to make the spot smaller until you can pitch and chip for a dime placed on the green. Make sure that you have a strong leading left hand before you pitch *over* objects such as bushes, etc. Allow the club to do the work.

5. Emphasize target direction—hit for general areas; then be quite specific and hit for exact spots.

6. Hit the ball using your left hand only; then repeat, using your right hand only.

7. Work for consistent timing and hit. Try to hit all the shots alike, establishing a sameness throughout the swing.

8. Practice hitting shots from the edge of the green and work out, hitting shots of varying lengths to a specific spot (Fig. 7.7).

9. *After* you have mastered the consistent shot with all the clubs, wedge through 3-iron, work with slowing and speeding tempo of the shot.

10. Mentally picture four different ways to hit each approach shot into the green. Choose the one that produces the most consistent results.

11. Practice hitting balls to different levels on a stairway, onto tables, over benches, and into chairs.

Fig. 7.7 Spot practice

8
Putting

Putting is by far the most "do it yourself" part of the golf game. There are certain mechanical moves that seem to help the majority of players execute the move with more consistency. In reality, regardless of how you choose to putt, the only thing that does count is getting the ball into the cup consistently and whatever works for *you* is best. About half of your shots in a regulation round are taken on the putting green, so you should spend a lot of practice time there. Because women tend to develop more small muscle control, women should be good putters. It seems that women have a keen sense of touch and feel which should help them to be fine putters. This is a place where your own individual style can blossom. Since there are hundreds of different putters available and many different putting styles, carefully choose one to fit your putting style.

The ideas presented here are those that make the physical stroke more repetitious—no one can teach you the feel, distance, and difficulty of each putt—it literally rests in your hands.

The Grip

1. Use the standard golf grip or reverse overlapping.

2. Many fine putters use the reverse overlap (Fig. 8.1) which allows the little finger on the right hand to be placed on the club and the index finger of the left hand to overlap the little finger of the right or even to extend down over two more fingers, if desired. This places the entire right hand on the club, giving more feel to the right hand.

3. Tension in the grip is important. Too much cuts down on the vital feel in the fingers. Too little tension causes varying speeds, deceleration, and loss of club head control at impact.

4. Where you place your hands on the grip of the club is your own choice.

Fig. 8.1 Overlapping grip—ball placed in center of stance

Fig. 8.2 Cross-handed grip
▼

Fig. 8.3 Separated grip—hands at top and bottom of club grip

Variations of grip

1. *Cross-handed* (Fig. 8.2). Put your right hand on the top of the grip, your left hand underneath—the reverse of the usual hand positions.

2. *Hands separated* (Fig. 8.3). Place your left hand on top of the grip of the club, your right hand at the bottom of the grip—leave a space between them.

Stance

1. Your body should be square or parallel to the line to the target—this includes feet, knees, hips, and shoulders.

2. The placement of the ball is optional. The majority of players play the ball off the center of the stance or off of the left toe (Fig. 8.4).

3. The weight placement is usually forward or equally distributed on the feet.

Fig. 8.4 Ball placement off front foot

Variations of stance

1. You may use either open or closed stance.
2. Face the hole. Place your left hand on top of club, back of hand toward target. Place your right hand down the shaft, palm facing target. Swing putter on normal path to target.

Body Position

1. Square your body to the line to the target.
2. Keep your eyes over the ball or behind the line to the target (Fig. 8.5).
3. Hold your body still during the putt (Fig. 8.6).
4. Hold your head still throughout the putt.

Fig. 8.5 Keep your eyes over the ball

Fig. 8.6 Putting sequence

Alignment

1. Study your putt while others are putting.
2. Line up your putt from behind, in front, and from the sides.
3. Get down behind the ball and look for contours and alignment.
4. You should note any grass patterns along the line to the cup.

   A. Shiny grass means the grass is growing towards the hole (with the ball direction)—the ball will roll faster over this area.

   B. Dull grass means the grass is growing against the ball direction— the ball will roll slower over this area.

   C. Cross-grain means you have to look for it and remember that as the ball dies it will break with the grain.

5. Try to see the imaginary line that the ball will follow.
6. Choose a point on your imaginary line and aim for it (Fig. 8.7).
7. Then, place the club behind the ball square to the spot on the line to the target.
8. If the hole is on a slant, putt for the high side of the cup.

Fig. 8.7 Right-to-left putt

9. Know which is your dominant eye.

   A. Using your index finger point to a ball. With both eyes open: align the finger with the ball. Close your right eye; open it. Then close your left eye and open it. The eye that, when closed, produces the greatest movement is the dominant eye. Take this dominance into consideration when aligning and placing your ball in your stance.

Variations of alignment

1. *Plumb-bob System*

   A. Stand about 6 to 12 feet directly behind the ball.

   B. Hold the putter near the top of the grip with the thumb and forefinger; hold it out at arms length; let it hang easy.

   C. Line the ball up with the cup down by the neck (hosel) of the club, then look up towards the top of the club. Close your weak eye. If the hole stays in line with the shaft, you have a straight putt (Fig. 8.8). If you see the hole on either side of the shaft, the ball will break towards the hole.

Fig. 8.8 Plumb-bob system

Putting Stroke in General

1. Keep your club face square to the target line throughout the stroke.

2. Keep your club low to the ground during the stroke.

3. There should be some acceleration of the club head as you hit the ball.
4. On short putts of two feet or under, use a short tapping action.
5. On a longer putt, use a more pendular stroke.
6. Try to maintain firm wrists throughout the stroke.

Variations of putting stroke

1. *Stroke Putt*

   A. Use either your standard grip or reverse overlap.

   B. Your back stroke and follow-through should be about the same length; if you take your putter blade one foot back, then follow through one foot forward (see Fig. 8.9) or, three feet back and three feet forward).

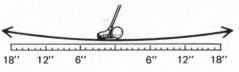

| 18" | 12" | 6" | | 6" | 12" | 18" |

Fig. 8.9 Stroke putt

Pendular swing	Should also be
6 inches back	6 inches forward
12 inches back	12 inches forward
18 inches back	18 inches forward

2. *Tap Putt*

    A. Use either your standard grip or reverse overlap.

    B. Make a short back swing and a short follow-through. Imagine you are trying to tap a tack into the back of the ball. Use a sharp, crisp, forward motion to the ball action—not a jab, but a tap—in a straight line to the cup. (See Fig. 8.10.)

Fig. 8.10 Stroke straight to target—straight back and straight forward

3. *Wrist Putting*

    A. Use your standard grip or reverse overlap.

    B. Hold your stance and body firm throughout the putt.

    C. Move your arms as little as possible throughout the swing.

    D. Take your club away from the ball and return it to the ball almost entirely with your wrists.

4. *Body Putting*

    A. Anchor your elbows firmly to your sides.

    B. Slide your hips and legs laterally toward the target as you make the stroke.

    C. Keep your putter blade square and on the target line.

    D. Resist temptation to rotate body as that will take putter blade inside of the intended line.

    E. Keep your head still.

    F. Grip club firmly.

    G. Use a square stance.

    H. Do not move hands and arms independently of the body.

    I. Move your body and arm as one unit.

5. *Texas Wedge* (Fig. 8.11)

    A. Use putter from off the green.

    B. Use standard grip and stance.

    C. Hit ball with a crisp, firm, sharp blow.

Fig. 8.11 Texas wedge

Mental Aspects

1. Practice to gain confidence in your stroke and feel.

2. On long putts, putt initially for a bushel basket size cup. Putt for distance, direction will come later.

3. Watch your ball if it goes beyond the cup. Note how it rolls and its speed. Use this knowledge on the return putt.

4. Be realistic—don't expect to knock all of your putts in. Spend the major portion of your practice time on the makeable ones from 1 foot to 12 feet.

5. Think positively—think how you are going to make the putt, *not* how you are going to miss it.

6. To estimate the distance from the ball to the cup on the putting green, visualize taking your putter blade back one inch for every foot you want the ball to go forward (Fig. 8.12).

Fig. 8.12   Distance chart

Take putter back	Ball travels
1 inch	1 foot
3 inches	3 feet
6 inches	6 feet

Stroke   Distance ball travels

1″ Ball goes 1'

3″ Ball goes 3'

6″ Ball goes 6'

Variations in Ground Contour

1. *Up-hill Putts*

   A. Play the ball an inch or so toward the higher foot.

   B. Use a firmer grip on the club so that it will produce a sharper, crisper stroke.

   C. Play for an imaginary hole that is beyond the actual cup.

2. *Down-hill Putt*

   A. Play the ball toward the higher foot.

   B. To slow the speed of the ball hit high on it, above the center, to start it toward the cup with less action on it.

   C. To deaden the action, hit the ball on the toe of your putter so that it does not take off very fast.

   D. Play for an imaginary hole in front of the actual cup.

   E. Grip the club gently, with little tension in your fingers.

   F. Try for a gentle, smooth, slower stroke.

3. *Right-to-Left Putt*

   A. Aim for a spot along your intended path slightly to the right of the hole.

   B. Hit directly for that spot, allowing the contour of the surface to curve the ball. Adapt the same concept for a *left-to-right* putt.

   C. Take the putter blade back on a slightly inward line and then stroke the ball forward, putting a right-to-left spin on the ball.

4. *Left-to-Right Putt*

   A. Aim for a spot along the intended path slightly to the left of the hole.

   B. Hit directly for that spot, allowing the contour of the surface to curve the ball.

   C. Take the putter blade back on an outward line away from the ball. Then stroke the ball forward, putting a left-to-right spin onto the ball.

General

1. On strange courses, practice on the putting surfaces before you play. Try to determine whether the greens are hard, soft, wet, dry, coarse, or fine. Use your feet and spikes when walking on the green to determine textures, hardness, etc.

2. Remember that firmly hit putts hold the line better and follow a straighter path than those hit with a gentle and soft stroke.

3. Watch green conditions in the morning when greens are wet. Be aware of condition during the round as greens become faster when they dry out.

4. When a large body of water is near the putting surface, the ball tends to break towards the water.

5. Near mountains, the ball tends to break away from the mountains.

Common Errors	Corrections
1. Tension in your hands.	Hit five shots with left hand; hit five shots with right hand; hit five shots with both hands.
2. Poor foot alignment.	Place club along foot line; sight down line; adjust feet.
3. Cutting across ball—outside-in shot.	Swing putter along target line. Place two clubs on green and putt between them.
4. Eyes outside of the intended target line.	Use putter to plumb line from bridge of nose to ball.
5. Eyes inside intended target line.	Adjust plumb line, as above. Move body closer to the ball or bend over more.
6. Misreading the green.	Get down low and survey putt from behind and sides of ball.
7. Pulling putts.	Swing arms in a more pendular motion.
8. Lack of feel.	Check hand tension. Try reverse-overlap grip.
9. Swinging inside target line on back and forward swings to make ball curve (an exception would be a slight curving motion on a right-to-left putt).	Pick out a spot on the line to the target. Putt straight toward the point with a straight stroke. Use two clubs to correct swing path.

Exercises

1. In the winter, putt on rugs at home.

2. Practice putting over floor boards or against baseboard to make sure your stroke is straight back and straight forward.

3. Putt between two clubs laid on the surface just the width of the putter apart. This exercise can be done using two yard sticks or string wrapped around tees at the end of the lines.

4. Practice putting with only one hand.

5. Start practice (regardless of length of practice time) with short 1-foot-length putts, then 2-, 3-, 6-, 15-, and 30-foot putts. Then work back down to 1 foot. Just before you play, be sure to practice with short putts to give you added confidence.

6. During *practice*, carry a spare ball and experiment after finishing each hole by rolling balls from different parts of the green to learn the rolls. Do this *only* on practice rounds when you will not delay play.

7. If you are having putting problems, change putters for a while. When you come back to your old putter it will feel better and you will have greater confidence.

9
Uneven Lies and Trouble Shots

Uneven lies and trouble shots are shots that call for imagination and flexibility. Your stance will probably not be on level ground as the ball may be lower or higher than your feet. One foot may be lower or higher than the other foot. The ball may be closer to you or further away from you than usual so, in these circumstances, the placement of the ball may interfere with the normal arc and balance of your swing. Below we discuss a few such possible shots and the basic method of dealing with them.

General Suggestions

1. Use a regular grip throughout unless directed otherwise.
2. Use regular width of stance for normal swing unless otherwise directed.

Uphill Shot

1. *Description*. The ball is lying on an uphill slope (see Fig. 9.1).
2. *Execution*
   A. Be aware of the contour of the ground.
   B. Use your standard grip and a square, shoulder-width stance.
   C. Always play the ball toward your highest foot.
   D. Use a less-lofted club than you would on a level lie.
   E. Always take a practice swing in order to visualize and feel the contour of the ground. Finish the swing high.
   F. Brace with the right foot and keep your weight more on the left foot in order to maintain balance, and lean into the hill.

Fig. 9.1   Uphill shot—ball placement and stance

Fig. 9.2   Downhill shot—ball placement and stance
▼

Fig. 9.3   Downhill/sidehill shot—execution

G. Let your swing follow the slope of the ground.

H. Shorten your swing to avoid overswinging and losing your balance.

I. Aim slightly to the right of target since there is a tendency for the ball to hook or be pulled.

Downhill Shot

1. *Description.* The ball is lying on a downhill slope (see Fig. 9.2).
2. *Execution*

   A. Use a more lofted club than you would for a level shot.

   B. Use your standard grip.

   C. Use a square, shoulder-width stance.

   D. Always play ball toward your highest foot.

   E. Always take a practice swing in order to visualize the shot and feel the contour of the ground.

   F. Swing back in a more upright plane than usual and follow through lower and longer.

   G. Brace with the left foot and keep your weight more on the right foot in order to maintain balance, and lean into the hill.

   H. Shorten your swing to avoid overswinging and losing your balance.

   I. Aim slightly to the left of target since the ball has a tendency to slice or be pushed.

Sidehill Lie—Feet Above Ball

1. *Description.* The ball is lying on a slope with the grade away from you and you are standing with your feet above the ball (see Fig. 9.3).

2. *Execution*

   A. Grip the club near the end.

   B. Use your regular grip.

   C. Assume a square stance, closer to the ball than usual.

   D. Play the ball near the center of the stance.

   E. Flex your knees slightly with your weight back over the heels in order to maintain balance, and lean into the hill.

   F. On extremely steep banks, use more chopping action than usual during the swing.

Sidehill Lie—Feet Below Ball

1. *Description.* The ball is lying on a slope with the grade towards you and you are standing with your feet lower than the ball (see Fig. 9.4).

2. *Execution*
   A. Shorten or choke up on the grip of the club.
   B. Use your standard grip.
   C. Use a square stance.
   D. Play the ball near the center of stance.
   E. Flex your knees slightly with your weight forward over the toes in order to maintain balance.
   F. Aim slightly to the right since ball has a tendency to hook or be pulled.
   G. Shorten your backswing to avoid overswinging and losing your balance.
   H. On extremely steep banks, use more chopping action than usual during the swing.

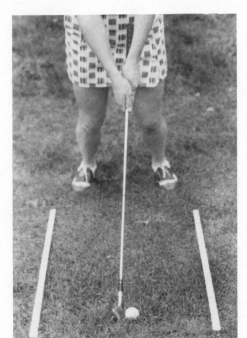

Fig. 9.4 Uphill/sidehill shot—execution

Steep Bank Shot

1. *Description.* The ball is in an uphill, downhill, or sidehill lie to an extreme degree of slope.

2. *Execution*

   A. Follow the points mentioned above for either an uphill or a downhill lie, depending upon the location of the ball.

   B. Use your standard grip.

   C. Use a square stance.

   D. Be aware of the contour of the ground.

   E. Since balance is very important in this type of shot, be careful not to overswing.

   F. Getting out must be your *prime* concern—even if you must aim straight out and not towards the hole.

   G. For banked shots where the grass is heavy, use a sand wedge, pitching wedge, or short iron.

   H. Play the ball near your higher foot. Hit through the ball with a chopping action in order to pop it out. Squeeze the ball between the club face and the bank. Hit it hard and very firmly.

Punch Shot

1. *Description.* A ball must travel a low trajectory under trees or branches or into the wind—a low "line-drive" shot.

2. *Execution*

   A. Use a less lofted club than usual.

   B. Use your standard grip.

   C. Choke down on the grip of the club.

   D. Use a square stance.

   E. Play the ball off your back foot.

   F. Close the club face.

   G. Position your hands ahead of the ball.

   H. Think of how you want the ball to go and make your swing accordingly.

   I. Hit down and through the ball.

   J. Keep your back swing and follow-through low.

Shot from the Rough

1. *Description.* The ball is lying in grass longer than that of the fairway.

2. *Execution (normal rough)*

    A. If you have a good lie, use a wood or long iron and play it like a fairway shot. Check lie very carefully.

    B. Use your regular grip.

    C. Use a square stance.

    D. Play ball center to back foot.

    E. Take a more upright back swing than usual and hit the ball with a descending blow.

3. *Variation (thick and heavy rough)*

    A. Use a short iron or wedge with a heavy flange.

    B. Take a more upright backswing than usual and use a chopping action to hit the ball.

    C. Play the ball center to off of back foot.

    D. Position your hands ahead of the ball and hood club face.

    E. Remember—a ball coming out of the rough will run more due to a lack of backspin.

    F. Your main concern should be to get out of the rough and position yourself for the next shot—always play lie over distance.

Shot from Bare Ground, Roads, or Rocks

1. *Description.* The ball is lying in a divot, on bare ground, in a road, on rocks, or on any hard surface (see Fig. 9.5).

2. *Execution*

    A. Use caution on all of these shots.

    B. Use your standard grip.

    C. Use a square stance.

    D. Keep your weight towards your left foot.

    E. Take a shorter, more upright backswing than usual.

    F. Do not overswing. This can cause you to lose your balance and slip.

    G. Pick the ball clean. Make contact with the ball first so that the club will not bounce off the hard surface.

Fig. 9.5 Hitting off bare ground, roads, or rocks

Water Shot

1. *Description.* The ball may be playable but is lying in one or two inches of water.

2. *Execution*
    A. Do not touch the water with the club on your backswing (two stroke penalty in stroke play—loss of hole in match play).
    B. Use your standard grip.
    C. Use a slightly open stance.
    D. Hit down on the ball as you would a buried sand shot.
    E. Hitting too far behind the ball can cause the clubhead to alter its path.
    F. When the club hits water it will lose its force at impact.

Backward Shot with Club Inverted

1. *Description.* A backward shot with the club inverted is used when ball is lying near a fence, tree, or some object and a penalty would be incurred to move the ball in order to hit it in the standard direction (Fig. 9.6).

2. *Execution*

   A. Choke down on the grip of the club.

   B. Use your standard grip.

   C. Use a square to slightly open stance, facing in the opposite direction from your normal stance.

   D. Use a short iron since this will yield a rounder and larger hitting surface.

   E. Play the ball center or towards back foot.

   F. Turn the club so that the toe is pointing down and the hitting surface of the club is towards the ball.

   G. Take a short waist-high backswing.

   H. With a sweeping action, hit the ball toward the target.

Fig. 9.6 Backward shot using inverted club

Backward Shot

1. *Description.* A backward shot is called for when a ball lying close to an object (tree, fence, etc.) prohibits address, stance, and swing in a normal position (Fig. 9.7).

2. *Execution*

   A. Grip the club with your right hand only. Face of club should face target.

   B. Use a back-to-target stance. Keep feet in close together, perpendicular to target line.

   C. Stand so that the ball is to the right of the center. Swing club away from target, waist high, with firm right arm.

   D. Accelerate club head toward the target. Swing to waist high behind you.

Fig. 9.7 Backward shot

Windshots

Upwind (into the wind)

1. *Description.* A low-trajectory, long-distance shot that holds its direction, is used when hitting into the wind. This shot is similar to a punch shot.

2. *Execution*

   A. Choke down on the grip of the club.

   B. Tee the ball lower.

   C. Use a less-lofted club than normal (choice depends on wind velocity).

   D. Use your regular grip.

   E. Use a square stance.

   F. Hood the club face.

   G. Play the ball center or towards back foot.

   H. Hit the ball firmly and crisply with a low follow through. Hold wrists and arms firm throughout shot.

Downwind (with the wind)

1. *Description.* A high-trajectory shot is used when the wind is at your back.

2. *Execution*

   A. Tee the ball higher.

   B. Use a more-lofted club than normal (choice depends on wind velocity).

   C. Play the ball towards your left foot.

   D. Use your standard grip.

   E. Use a square stance.

   F. Finish your swing high.

Crosswind

1. *Description.* A crosswind shot is used to compensate for the wind blowing from either direction across your line of flight.

2. *Execution*

   A. Allow for the wind-effect on the flight path of your ball—line up accordingly with the target.

   B. Use a less-lofted club to diminish the effect of the wind on the shot.

C. Use one club more than normal, depending upon the velocity of the wind.

D. Use your standard grip.

E. Use a square stance.

F. Use a normal swing.

G. Remember that if you hook in a left crosswind or slice in a right crosswind, the wind will magnify your mistake.

Under-Tree Shot

1. *Description.* To remove the ball from an under-tree lie, a shot with a low trajectory (approximately 5 feet off the ground) is needed.

2. *Execution*

A. Play the ball as you would a punch shot or into-the-wind shot.

B. Choke down on the grip of the club.

C. Use your regular grip.

D. Use a square stance.

E. Play the ball towards your right foot.

F. Hood a long iron for a low trajectory (even a putter may be used).

G. Use a firm wrist action throughout the shot.

H. Keep backswing and follow-through low—no more than waist high on either side.

I. Use a driver when maximum distance is necessary.

J. When you are under very low branches, widen your stance to the very maximum. This will lower your entire body. Almost do the splits. Then your whole swing will be very flat and low under the branches.

10
Sand Shots

In executing sand shots, it is important to remember that the grip, extension of arms, body motion, and other swing principles are basically the same as for shots on the fairway. There are three basic shots to get you out of a bunker—a putt, a regular chip, and an explosion. When a deep bunker is near the green, the best method of getting out is to blast or explode the ball out. This is done by hitting the sand behind the ball, preferably with a heavy-flanged sand wedge. The sand serves as a cushion between the clubhead and ball reducing the distance the ball normally would travel off a blow of equal force. When you get into the sand, don't panic! Just say, "If I got in here, I'll get out." Practice that thought of getting out; closeness to the hole will come later.

General Suggestions

1. Before you enter the trap, survey the situation.
2. Select the appropriate club (a putter, sand wedge, pitching wedge, or short iron).
3. As you enter the sand, feel the texture of the sand with your feet.*
4. Use your standard grip.
5. Wiggle your feet into the sand to get a good firm open stance. Line up about 45° left of the target for a sand shot. Have the club face open and swing with a spanking action.
6. Restrict your pivot.
7. Swing slowly and deliberately, swinging to the finish.

* If the sand is deep and powdery, usually an explosion shot is used. If the sand is wet, coarse, or shallow, the ball will sit up more and you can use a pick-chip-like shot.

Fig. 10.1   Explosion shot

8. Do not sole your club in the sand (two stroke penalty in stroke play—loss of hole in match play).
9. Be composed.

Explosion Shot

This type of shot is usually played when the trap is near a green which has an embankment (Fig. 10.1).

1. Use your sand wedge.
2. Choke down on the club with standard grip.
3. Wiggle your feet into the sand.
4. Use an open stance.
5. Place the ball center-to-forward towards your left foot.
6. Open your club face slightly.
7. If right-handed, aim a little left of target (if left-handed, aim a little right of target).
8. Focus on and try to hit a point about one to two inches behind the ball.
9. Swing in a more upright plane, cutting across the line, swinging slightly outside-in. Use about a ¾ swing.
10. Spank the sand with the flange of the club.
11. Finish the shot. Remember to follow through.

Variations

1. *Uphill Lies in Sand Traps*
   A. Use a sand wedge or a pitching wedge when close to the green. Use a less-lofted club when hitting from a fairway trap.
   B. Use your regular grip.
   C. Use a square to slightly open stance.
   D. Play the ball about one inch behind the normal ball position for an uphill lie.
   E. Rest your weight on your right foot.
   F. Hit the sand slightly closer to the ball than a normal hit.
   G. Swing to the contour of the ground.

2. *Buried Uphill Lie* (Fig. 10.2)

   A. For a deeply buried ball, use a sand wedge or possibly a nine iron or pitching wedge to cut into sand.

   B. Use your regular grip.

   C. Use a square to slightly open stance.

   D. Keep your weight back on the right foot.

   E. Play the ball near your front (left) foot.

   F. Hit as closely to the ball as possible with a descending chopping blow.

   G. Take the club slightly outside the line of flight.

3. *Downhill Lies in Sand Traps*

   A. Use a sand wedge.

   B. Use your regular grip.

   C. Use a square to slightly open stance.

   D. Play the ball off the right heel.

   E. Keep your weight on the left foot.

   F. Swing the club in a more upright arc than usual.

   G. Hit the sand about an inch behind the ball.

4. *Buried Downhill Lies*

   A. Use a sand wedge, nine iron, or pitching wedge.

   B. Use your regular grip.

   C. Use a square to slightly open stance.

   D. Play the ball off your right heel.

   E. Keep your weight on your left foot.

5. *Wet Sand Lies* (This type of sand shot is used when the sand is wet and hard packed.)

   A. Use your regular grip.

   B. Use a slightly open stance.

   C. Play the ball off or near the back foot.

   D. Since the ball is usually sitting up more than in other sand situations, a chip-type shot can be used.

   E. Wrists should be firm throughout this shot since when the club hits the sand it meets with much resistance.

   F. Pick the ball off the sand, hitting the ball first as in a chip shot.

Fig. 10.2 Buried lie in sand

Chip Shot

This type of shot is used out of a shallow bunker with a good lie.

1. Use your standard grip.
2. Use either an 8-iron, 9-iron, or pitching wedge.
3. Use a square or slightly open stance.
4. Open or square the club face, depending upon particular shot and the distance needed.
5. Play the ball from in the center to off the right foot.
6. Hit through the shot as if playing off the turf.
7. Hit the ball first, taking little or no sand.

Distance Sand Shot

This type of shot is used when sand traps are far from the green.

1. Choose one club longer than you would ordinarily use.
2. Choose a club suited to your lie before you consider distance.
3. Use a club with enough loft to clear the lip of the trap.
4. Use your standard grip.
5. Wiggle your feet into sand since you will be taking a fuller swing at the ball.
6. Keep your weight even to maintain balance.
7. Do not overswing, or you will lose your footing and balance.

Putting Out of Trap

This type of shot (Fig. 10.3) is used when the lip is very shallow or there is no lip at all.

1. Use your putter.
2. Use your putting grip.

Fig. 10.3 Putting out of trap

3. Use a square to slightly open stance.

4. Play the ball off your right foot.

5. Strike the ball first. Try to hit little or no sand.

6. Hit the ball hard enough to go through the sand and over whatever ground is necessary to reach the green.

7. Allow for extra run since the ball will usually run out in a low trajectory.

Buried Shots

This type of shot is used when the ball is covered with sand.

1. Use your standard grip.

2. Square or hood your club face.

3. Play ball from center to right foot.

4. Hit down on the ball with a chopping action.

5. Allow for extra run since the ball will come out with a low trajectory and very little backspin.

6. Use a sand wedge most of the time; however, if the ball is deeply buried, either a nine iron or a pitching wedge with a thin flange can cut more deeply into the sand due to its sharper cutting surface.

Common Errors (for normal explosion shot)	Corrections
1. Club face square to hooded.	Keep club face square to open.
2. Ball position back.	Have ball centered to forward.
3. Club face back too far on the inside.	Take club back slightly on an outside line.
4. Swaying, moving off the ball.	Hold head steady; maintain balance by digging feet into sand deeper.
5. Lack of wrist action—arms too firm.	Use soft, lazy, wristy-type swing.
6. Casting from the top; hitting too soon; digging into the sand.	Lead with the left side and pull arms closer toward the body.
7 Weight staying on the back foot after completion of swing.	Maintain balance; shift weight towards left foot.
8. Losing balance.	Wiggle feet into sand; develop a downward, inward feeling into the sand.
9. Trying to slug ball out of the sand; jumping at ball; excess body action.	Maintain balance and restrict body action; finish the shot; follow through.
10. Picking, putting or chip variation; hitting the sand before the ball.	Strike ball first, then sand. Imagine hitting a normal shot without the sand.

Practice Suggestions

1. Hit the sand and feel as if you are throwing sand out of the trap with the club—this helps develop a spanking sensation. Then, duplicate that feeling using a ball.
2. Before entering the trap, survey the trap, analyze the shot, and select the club for the shot.
3. Get into the sand and check the texture of the sand with your feet. Then recheck your club selection.
4. Select a speck or spot to aim at one to two inches behind the ball so that you hit the sand before you hit the ball when practicing explosion shot.
5. Place your feet in the sand; wiggle. Create a mental picture of the shot, then execute it.
6. Draw a line about two inches behind a row of balls in the sand. (See Fig. 10.4.) Hit the line, moving up along the line, hitting the balls as you go, but always making contact with the line first—then with the ball.
7. Draw an egg-shaped circle in the sand and practice hitting all of the sand out of the trap. Then put a ball in the center of the oval-shaped mark and practice hitting it out.

Fig. 10.4 Basic drill for blast shot

11
Rules

A thorough understanding of the rules of golf is necessary for all players, whether they be tournament competitors or "once a week" golfers. Having this knowledge makes it possible for you to know the penalties involved in given situations.

Another and often overlooked aspect of the rules is the way in which they may *help* you and save you strokes. The standard U.S.G.A. Rules Book, which you should carry in your golf bag, can seem like an overwhelmingly complicated lawyer's manual. The three-inch thick rules-interpretation volume seems even more complicated. The following chart is a summary of the most commonly used rules and their penalties for stroke and match play. A column has been added to show the privileges each rule gives to the player. This is not an attempt to duplicate the U.S.G.A. Rules Book. You, as an advanced player, must know where and how to obtain a more detailed version of the rules.

General Rules

(Applicable anywhere on the course)

Rules	Advantages and General Information
1. You may carry up to 14 clubs in your bag. Penalty: For carrying extra clubs: *Stroke.* Two strokes for each hole at which the violation occurred; maximum penalty per round—four strokes *Match.* Loss of hole at which violation occurred; maximum penalty per round—two lost holes	You may choose those clubs that you think will be best for the course conditions that day—no more than 14.

Rules	Advantages and General Information
2. You must play the same ball with which you started.	You may identify a ball at any time except in a hazard.

Penalty: For playing wrong ball:

Stroke. Two stroke penalty

Match. Loss of hole

| 3. You may replace a damaged ball.

Penalty: If you fail to do it in the presence of your opponent or scorer:

Stroke. Two strokes

Match. Loss of hole | You should replace a ball that has been scarred whenever it would influence the play; however, you must first get the approval of your opponent to replace the damaged ball. Do not tee off with damaged balls. |

| 4. You may clean your ball only when you remove it from a water hazard, an obstruction, or an unplayable lie, when playing under winter rules, when the ground is under repair, when the ball lies in casual water, and when it is on the green. | Keep your ball clean. Remove mud or debris as often as possible—they affect the flight of the ball. You must *lift* the ball to clean it. |

Penalty: For unauthorized cleaning:

Stroke. Two strokes

Match. Loss of hole

| 5. You must play in turn.

Penalty: For playing out of turn:

Stroke. No penalty

Match. Opponent may recall shot and require that you play it again. | Pay attention—you may gain or lose an advantage by playing out of turn. |

| 6. You may receive advice *only* from your partner or caddie.

Penalty: For asking unauthorized advice:

Stroke. Two strokes

Match. Loss of hole | Ask your partner for advice on difficult shots. Compare his thoughts with your own. Ask your caddie's advice about fairway positions, green rolls, and club choices. |

From the Tee to the Green

Rules	Advantages and General Information
1. When teeing your ball, you must tee the ball in line with the markers	Use the two clubs distance behind the markers to gain better footing or angle

Rules	Advantages and General Information

or within an area two club lengths behind them (measured using longest club).

Penalty: For teeing outside the teeing area:

Stroke. You must count both illegal stroke and subsequent teeing stroke played within teeing ground. Breach of rule causes disqualification.

Match. Opponent may immediately require you to replay shot without penalty.

on the shot, or to help decide which club to use.

2. If you can't move an obstruction away from your ball, you may move your ball away from such obstructions as pipes, paper, rakes, hoses, shelters, buildings, benches, fountains, pebbles, dead leaves, etc.

If you know the obstructions from which you may and may not move, it may save you an unplayable-lie penalty and allow you a free drop.

Penalty: For moving ball improperly away from obstruction:

Stroke. Breach—two strokes

Match. Loss of hole

No penalty is incurred if the ball is moved within two club lengths of that outside margin of the obstruction nearest to the spot where the ball lay. Ball may not be moved nearer the hole.

3. You may remove your ball from casual water, ground under repair, or a hole burrowed by an animal.

Knowing the course and the local rules application may save you strokes and give you a better lie and position.

Penalty: No Penalty:

Breach of rule:

Penalty:

Stroke. Two strokes

Match. Loss of hole

4. Any attempt to hit the ball counts as one stroke.

Penalty: For missing ball:

Stroke: No penalty—but if you swing and *miss*, it counts as one stroke.

Match: No penalty—but if you swing and *miss*, it counts as one stroke.

Take your practice swings well away from the hitting area. Place your club carefully so that the ball does not accidentally move and cost you a stroke.

Rules

5. Hitting the ball out of bounds.

Penalty: For hitting out of bounds:

Stroke. Loss of stroke and distance

Match. Loss of stroke and distance

6. Losing ball outside of a hazard.

Penalty: For lost ball:

Stroke. Loss of stroke and distance.

Match. Loss of stroke and distance.

7. You may declare a ball unplayable any time *you* want—it is *your* decision.

Penalty: For unplayable lie:

Stroke.

    i) Loss of stroke and distance

    ii) Move the ball two club lengths from the spot where it lies (not nearer the hole) adding one stroke

    iii) Take the ball back behind the spot where it lies. Keeping the spot between you and the hole. There is no limit to how far back you may go. One stroke penalty

If options ii or iii are applied in a bunker, the ball must be dropped in the bunker.

Match. Same as stroke penalty

8. Hitting the ball into the water directly in front of you.

Penalty: For removing the ball from the water:

Stroke: One stroke penalty; bring ball directly back of spot as far back as you want, keeping spot where it last crossed the margin of the hazard between you

Advantages and General Information

Play a provisional ball when there is any doubt that the ball may be out of bounds. Know your course and play cautiously on potential out-of-bounds holes.

If you think there is any chance that your ball is lost, play a provisional ball. When you play the provisional ball: (1) you may abandon the original ball before searching; (2) you may not play the provisional ball beyond the point where the original ball lies or is in the way. Take mental note of the position of the ball as soon as you hit it. If the ball was teed, you may retee it. You are allowed five minutes to look for your ball. Let faster players go through.

Study all three choices. Use your driver when measuring—it's the longest club. You may *not* hit a provisional ball for an unplayable lie.

Remember if the stroke and distance penalty is chosen and the shot *was* originally teed, it may be reteed.

You may play the ball from the water if *you* want; do not touch the water with your club at address or as you start your swing—it is a two stroke penalty; remember the banks of the hazard extend vertically upward from the marked edge, or vertically upward from the water if not marked. You may go back as

Rules | **Advantages and General Information**

and the flag; or you may instead go back as far as you want to the original spot, teeing if the stroke was teed

Match: Same as stroke penalty

9. Hitting the ball into water that is parallel or lateral to your fairway.

Penalty

Stroke.

i) You may take a two club-length drop, on either side of the hazard, at the point where the ball entered the hazard. One-stroke penalty.

ii) You may move as far back as you wish, but you must keep the spot where the ball last crossed the margin between you and the hole. One stroke penalty.

iii) You may go back to the spot where the ball was originally played, teeing it if it was teed. One-stroke penalty.

Match. Same as stroke penalty

far as you want, so get a good lie. A ball that is *lost* in the water takes a water penalty.

Weigh all the possibilities carefully —one may give you a definite advantage. Know at which points the water is parallel or lateral to the fairway.

In a Hazard

Rules | **Advantages and General Information**

1. Obstructions in a hazard

   A. Penalty: For removing ball from obstruction in a hazard:

Stroke: No penalty. Ball may be moved two club lengths from the spot if the obstruction interferes with the stance, stroke, or backswing. It may not be measured over, through, or under the obstruction. Ball must stay in the hazard.

Breach of rule:

Stroke: Two strokes

Match: Loss of hole

You may remove the ball from a hazard, but you must take a one stroke penalty; you may move artificial objects such as bottles, rakes, cigar butts, etc. away from your ball; know the obstructions on your course; you may move your ball from, for instance, a bridge and its supports if the supports are not part of the bank. Artificially surfaced banks or walls are *not* obstructions.

Rules   **Advantages and General Information**

2. You may not ground your club in the sand.

Penalty: For grounding club in trap:

Stroke. Two strokes

Match. Loss of hole

Test the sand with your feet as you take your stance. Check its texture. Do not take a practice swing anywhere in the trap—outside the trap, you may ground your club in the grass. If your ball is buried, you may fleck only as much sand off the ball as is necessary to find it. Be sure to rake the trap after you leave.

Hitting Onto the Green

Rules   **Advantages and General Information**

1. If your ball is not on the green surface when you start to hit and you hit either the flag or another ball that is lying on the green.

Penalty

Stroke. No penalty

Match. No penalty

As long as you are playing from off the green surface, you may hit the pin, even if you are using a putter. Ask your opponent to remove his or her ball if it interferes with your line. You may leave your opponent's ball where it lies if it is to your advantage to do so. If your ball is in someone else's line, mark it correctly. Place a coin no bigger than a nickel directly behind the ball, then pick up the ball. Replace it in the same manner. If your coin is in someone else's line to the cup, move the coin to the right or left of the line using your putter blade as a measure. Replace the coin in its original spot before replacing the ball. Then putt.

On the Green

Rules   **Advantages and General Information**

1. You may clean your ball on the green. In match, you must replace it immediately.

Penalty: For cleaning ball:

Stroke. No penalty

Match. No penalty

Keep your ball clean at all times. Dirt influences the roll of the ball. Be sure to replace the ball in its exact spot. Mark your ball by placing a small coin or marker directly behind the ball (as above) when picking it up to clean it.

2. You may repair ball marks made on the green. You may not repair spike marks or any other mark on the surface.

Check your line and fix ball marks. Except for ball marks, do not press down the line to your ball in any way. You may remove twigs, leaves, and debris from your line.

Rules   **Advantages and General Information**

Penalty: For repairing marks other than ball marks:

Stroke. Two strokes

Match. Loss of hole

3. You may not hit someone else's ball when you are making a stroke from the putting surface.

Penalty: For hitting someone else's ball:

Stroke. Two-stroke penalty

Match. No penalty for hitting opponents ball on putting surface. Opponent may return ball to original spot or leave it where it now lies.

4. You may not hit flag or flag attendant when stroking from putting surface.

Penalty: For hitting flag or attendant:

Stroke. Two-stroke penalty.

Match. Loss of hole

Have opponent mark his ball if it will interfere with your putt. Have the pin loose before you putt and attended when you are putting from the putting surface.

12
Courtesies

This is the part of the game where a player can really be conspicuous. If you have not learned the courtesies, you will feel out of place as soon as you walk onto the course. Certain manners are expected of you whether you are playing or watching a golf match. Learn these early and well, for in most cases you are not invited to play because of your golfing skill, but for the pleasure of your company. You will be acceptable playing with anyone of any skill level if you know and apply the "Do's and Don'ts" of golfing manners.

Before Play

1. Call and arrange a game with a group.
2. Call for starting times, if necessary. Make arrangements for caddies or carts if you plan to use them.
3. Select comfortable, conservative clothes, and low-heeled shoes such as tennis or golf shoes.
4. When you arrive—check in at the pro shop, pay green fees and complete your caddie or cart arrangements.
5. Check the local rules on the back of the score card.
6. Check your bag to be sure that you have no more than 14 clubs. Each player should have his own bag and clubs.

General Rules

1. Stand quietly and motionless whenever anyone is hitting.
2. Keep practice swings to a minimum.
3. Watch where your fellow players' shots have landed. Mark the spot by reference to a fixed object.

4. *Play golf* on the course—don't teach others on the course. Socialize, but don't turn it into a social gab-fest.
5. Be courteous and a good sport—don't forget to compliment all the good shots made by each player.
6. Move quickly between shots.

On the Tee

1. Identify your own golf ball.
2. Place your golf bag off of the teeing section.
3. Stand to the right of the tee and well back of the markers.
4. On the first tee, flip a coin to see who has the honor (teeing first).
5. Stand quietly and motionless while others are hitting.
6. Pick up tee and replace divots, if necessary.
7. On the second through the eighteenth tee, the player who scored lowest on the previous hole goes first. If the score is tied, the order between the tied players reverts to that in which they teed off on the previous hole.
8. Play provisional balls after others have hit.
9. Move quickly between shots.

From the Tee to the Green

1. The ball farthest from the hole is hit first, both on and off the green.
2. Be sure there is no one ahead of you and that all other players are well beyond your range before you hit. Don't drive the ball into other groups on the fairway or on the green.
3. Help others in the group locate their balls.
4. Think about club selection and type of shot while you walk or ride to your ball.
5. Replace your divots.
6. Tell other players if you plan to hit a provisional ball and for what reason.
7. Use the word "fore" to warn other players on the course if your ball is headed in their direction.
8. When you hit a ball into another fairway, you are the intruder—the other group has the right-of-way.
9. Allow faster players to play through your group on to the next hole.

10. Place bags off of the green surface.
11. Move quickly between shots.

In Sand Traps

1. Place your bag or cart outside of the trap.
2. Don't walk through the trap unless you are hitting your shot.
3. Rake the sand trap when you leave; place rake outside of trap when you have finished raking it.
4. Move quickly between shots.

On the Green

1. Repair the marks made by the balls.*
2. The player closest to the pin holds it for the other players while they putt and removes the pin when it is no longer needed to line up putt.
3. Lay the pin down gently off of the green surface.
4. Study and line up your putt while others are putting.
5. Take the ball out of the cup as soon as it goes in.
6. The first player to finish his putt should pick up the flag and be ready to replace it as soon as the last player in the group has holed out.
7. Keep your shadow off of the putting line of the other players.
8. Step over and not on the line of other players' putts.
9. Leave the green together.
10. If your ball is in someone else's line, mark your ball correctly. Place a coin no bigger than a nickel directly behind the ball and then pick up the ball. Replace it in the same manner. If your coin is in someone else's line to the cup, move the coin right or left of the line using your putter blade as a measure. Replace the coin in its original spot before replacing the ball, and then putt.
11. You must putt with the same ball with which you teed off unless it has been lost or damaged.
12. Settle all disputes before you tee off on the next tee.
13. Count your score and mark the card off of the green.
14. Move quickly between shots.

*Use a wooden tee or divot fixer to dig around the edge of the mark, raising the depressed area. Pull the grass back to the original position and step gently or tap down with your putter head to smooth out the mark.

Carts

1. Know how to operate your cart.
2. Carts should come no nearer than 30 feet to the tees and greens.
3. Follow cart paths and directional signals.
4. Drive around wet areas.
5. Keep feet in the cart; don't hang out of the cart.
6. Drive cart carefully, avoiding hazards and steep hills.
7. Set brakes on the cart when stopping.
8. Don't overload the cart.

Caddies

1. Caddies are few and far between, but if you have a caddie, treat him as a human being.
2. Make your golf bag as light as possible.
3. Be courteous at all times.
4. Instruct your caddie on areas of special interest that apply to your game that day, such as flag attendance, club selection, hazards, and rules.
5. Pay caddie fees. Tip according to job done—poor, good, excellent.

13
Safety

Besides the characteristic "fore" that is shouted on the golf course to warn of danger, little is said about safety factors on the course. Yet insurance companies' figures rank golf only behind boxing and football for the number of injuries occurring each year. Whether you are playing by yourself or in a group, safety should be one of your prime concerns. Out-of-doors, on the course, the ball becomes the missile which causes the most injuries. Indoors, the club takes the role of the "one to watch." Stay alert to the general over-all picture and observe the precautions below.

General

1. Stay in line with other hitters.
2. Hit into areas where stray shots will do no damage.
3. When working out with others, be sure you know where and when they plan to hit.
4. Place your practice balls behind and to the right of your hitting station.
5. Don't walk near others who are practicing. Stay at your own station.

On the Course

1. Check to see that all players are out of your hitting range both on the fairway and on the green.
2. Take practice swings well away from other players.
3. Stand to the right side, and well out of the range, of others that are hitting on the tee.

4. Call "fore" if you should accidently hit a ball toward anyone.

5. Cover your head and duck immediately if you hear the word "fore". Look around and say what you want *after* the ball has landed.

6. Never walk out in front or ahead of the hitter.

7. Make sure that caddies and carts are well out of swinging range.

8. When hitting near trees, be aware of the possibility of ricochet shots and their danger.

9. In deep rough or hazards, watch out for roots and rocks under the ball.

10. When allowing other groups to go through, move to the sides of the fairway well out of range of their shots. If possible, stand close to a tree so its trunk is between you and the hitter.

11. Do not lick golf balls. They may have picked up harmful chemicals from the green and fairways.

On the Practice Range

1. Use line formations and be far enough apart that there will be no danger when you swing. Have at least five giant steps between you and the next player.

2. Wait for the signal so that everyone retrieves the balls at the same time.

3. When there is a group of people hitting balls, do not move out of your own station. Be especially careful when helping others. Make sure you know what the other person is planning to do.

4. When chipping around the practice green, use caution when others are opposite you on the green.

Indoor Practice

1. Use a line formation for hitting.

2. Use soft plastic balls for hitting.

3. Hit balls toward walls that will not be damaged if a club should be thrown during the follow through.

4. Have towels available to dry hands.

5. Keep the room temperature cool to prevent excessive perspiration.

6. Hit hard balls close to or inside of a net.

7. Hit Mac-Col balls or short rebound balls close to a solid wall. Although they don't ricochet, they are still very dangerous going forward.

8. Space at least five giant steps between mats for practice during full swing.

9. Periodically check your clubs for possible loose heads or slippery grips.

10. Buy your clubs from reliable manufacturers to assure yourself of good quality. That will ensure such things as tight club heads, strong shafts, and grips that will not wear quickly and become loose in your hands.

Weather

1. Suspend play when there is lightning.

2. Do not wait under trees or near clubs during a storm.

3. Go to shelter areas to wait for acceptable weather.

4. Keep hands and club grips dry.

4. Wear spiked shoes in wet weather.

6. Avoid banks and hills when ground is wet.

7. Do not use steel-shafted umbrellas.

8. Be cautious on extremely hot days. Know the symptoms of heat stroke. Use drinking fountains to cool your face, neck, arms, wrists, and legs.

Carts

1. Check cart to see that it is operating correctly. Check brakes, steering, and electrical connections. Know how it works.

2. *Do not* let children operate carts.

3. Don't overload carts.

4. Avoid steep banks and hills.

5. Avoid soft areas and slippery surfaces.

6. Do not speed in carts.

7. Drive cart carefully, avoiding hazards.

8. Set brake on cart when stopping.

14
Equipment

To many people, having fancy equipment and the right clothes provide one of the main reasons for playing golf—that is, basically, to be seen. Truly these would seem to be legitimate reasons—to be part of a group and to just plain look good. Not everyone can be a champion and play near-par golf. To take a four-hour walk with friends that you enjoy—and to do this on a beautifully manicured park looking your sporty best —seems like as good a reason as any for you to be there. If you like your equipment, you will feel that you have fourteen friends in your bag playing the shots with your help. There are considerable varieties in selections of golf equipment. Think about some of these when you make your choice.

Clubs

1. Consider your overall body size and strength in comparison with other men or women, as well as your personal preferences.
    A. How long are your arms?
    B. What size are your hands?
    C. What general price do you want to pay?
    D. How many clubs do you want?
    E. What type of clubs do you have now?
    F. What are your personal choices in color, wood stains, etc.?
2. The following are the standard ranges in clubs for *men*.
    A. Starter sets (Fig. 14.1) include 1- and 3-woods, 3-, 5-, 7-, 9-irons, and a putter.
    B. The lengths of the woods vary from between 43½ and 43 inches for the driver to about 41¼ inches for a 5-wood.

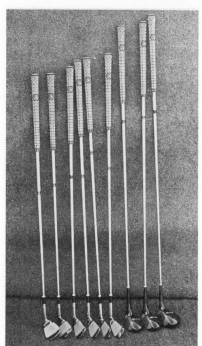

Fig. 14.1 Starter Set Plus

Fig. 14.2 Complete set of clubs

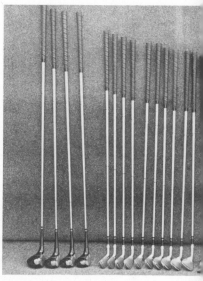

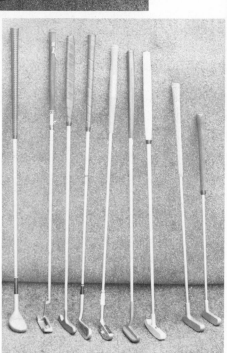

Fig. 14.3 Putters

     i) The shafts are stiff, regular, and soft or flexible, made of steel, light-weight steel, aluminum, or graphite.

     ii) Grips are leather, composition, or rubber.

     iii) The heads are made of plastic or of solid or laminated wood.

     iv) Swing weights range from D0 to D6 with the average being D2.

     v) Lofts on woods are close to eleven on a driver and vary two to three degrees per club.

     vi) Standard grip size 2½ inches down the shaft is $^{28}/_{32}$ tapered to $^{25}/_{32}$ at a point 5½ inches down the shaft.

     vii) Lie of the wood is 56° and it usually varies one degree per club.

     viii) Face of the club is straight—to hook lie varies from ½ to ¼ degree per club.

  C. Complete sets usually include four woods and 1-, 3-, 4-, 5-, and 9-irons (see Fig. 14.2).

     i) Irons usually include a 2-iron through a 9-iron plus a pitching wedge, a sand wedge, and a putter. (A variety of putters is shown in Fig. 14.3.)

       a) Lengths vary from 38½ inches for a 2-iron to 35½ inches for a 9-iron.

       b) Grips and swing weights are the same as for woods.

       c) Lie varies one to two from the standard 57° 2-iron.

     ii) Although, during play, your choice of clubs may not exceed the 14-club limit, you may purchase as many as you want and play with any combination of 14 clubs that you feel suit the conditions of a given round.

3. Standard clubs for *women* usually have the following features:

  A. A standard starter set includes 1- and 3-woods, and 3-, 5-, 7-, and 9-irons as well as a putter.

     i) Shafts are regular and flexible, made of steel, lightweight steel, aluminum, and/or graphite.

     ii) Standard grips for women are smaller than those for men. Grips may be $^{1}/_{32}$ oversize or undersize.

     iii) Woods are made of solid wood, laminated wood, or plastic.

     iv) Swing weights vary from C4 to D0, averaging C8.

     v) Standard irons are 2- to 9-irons, with a pitching wedge, a sand wedge, and a putter.

       a) Clubs come in graduated lengths: a 2-iron is usually 37½ inches long; a 9-iron, 35½ inches.

    B. A full set of clubs usually includes 1-, 3-, 4-, and 5-woods, 2-, 3-, 4-, 5-, 6-, 7-, and 9-irons, a pitching wedge, a sand wedge, and a putter.

    C. Although you may not carry more than 14 clubs during play, you may purchase any number.

4. Clubs are made in store lines and pro-shop lines.

    A. Very seldom will they be mixed.

    B. Pro lines are usually available only through pro shops, or in stores that hire golf professionals.

    C. You can purchase inexpensive to expensive lines in either type of line.

5. The overall weight of a man's club is greater than that of a lady's club.

    A. A man's driver usually weighs 13 ounces, while the average lady's driver is 12 ounces.

        i) When the average woman swings a man's club with its extra weight, the club-head speed diminishes since she does not have sufficient weight and strength to swing the extra weight as fast as she would a lady's club.

        ii) A woman will get faster club-head speed using a ladies' club—a faster club-head speed yields greater distance.

6. Junior clubs have less length, size, and weight. Their grip is even smaller than ladies.

    A. These are made especially for small children and aid their game until they have grown sufficiently to warrant their using regular size clubs.

    B. They are also ideal for very small, petite women.

    C. It is inadvisable to cut down an adult set since this changes so many of the characteristics of the club.

7. Choosing Clubs:

    A. Make a fist. Measure how far your knuckles are from the floor. The distance is approximately 29" for the average woman and about 30" for the standard arm length to the knuckles for the average man. If your arms hang closer to the ground, use shorter clubs. If they hang higher than normal, use longer clubs.

    B. If you have medium-sized hands, use a standard grip. Undersized grips are for smaller hands while larger hands require an oversized grip.

Balls

1. Construction:
   A. Solid balls—plastic or rubber—one piece
   B. Solid balls—with a cover of tough rubber
   C. Wound balls—rubber band type construction. (Centers are made of steel, liquid, or a small solid rubber ball.)

2. Standard balls have compression ratings (squeezability) of 80, 90, or 100 which are usually denoted by color coding. Red lettering and red numbers = 80; black lettering and red numbers = 90; black lettering and black numbers =100.
   A. Compression of the ball is varied by the degree of tightness used in winding of the rubber bands or by the flexibility of the solid material.
   B. Women usually use the 80 and 90 compression balls while men use the 90 and 100 compression balls. Because men are, on the average, larger, heavier, and stronger than women, they usually exert greater force in hitting the ball and can compress the ball more.
   C. Balls are numbered 1 through 8 so that the same brand ball may be used by several players, each playing a different number.

3. Aerodynamically, the dimples on the ball enable it to be lifted into flight like an airplane wing.

4. Prices vary.
   A. Lower-priced balls generally have a tougher cover.
   B. Everything about an expensive ball is well made and aerodynamically perfect. The covers are generally thinner than those on a low-priced ball.
   C. "Bargain" balls are not always true in flight nor accurate in compressability and distance obtained.
   D. Select balls from name manufacturers for quality results.

5. Mark balls with your own name for easy identification.

6. Use light-weight plastic balls for indoor use.

7. For indoor practice, consider the use of the Mac-Col ball. It has the weight and heavy feel of a regular ball but does not rebound off of a wall. It just hits and rolls back. They may be purchased from Bucol Rubber Company, Oxford, Ohio.

Gloves

1. Gloves come in wide varieties of colors, shapes, and both men's and women's regular hand sizes (Fig. 14.4).

2. Right-handed players wear gloves on their left hands.

3. Wearing a glove is optional. They are generally worn by players whose hands perspire or who have tender skin on their hands. Many feel they get a better grip on the club when wearing a glove.

4. Thinner leather allows for greater transmission of feel.

5. Ball markers may be attached to some of the gloves.

6. In cold, wet weather, wear white cotton gloves to keep your hands warm and dry.

7. Store gloves in a plastic container or jar to keep leather soft and dry.

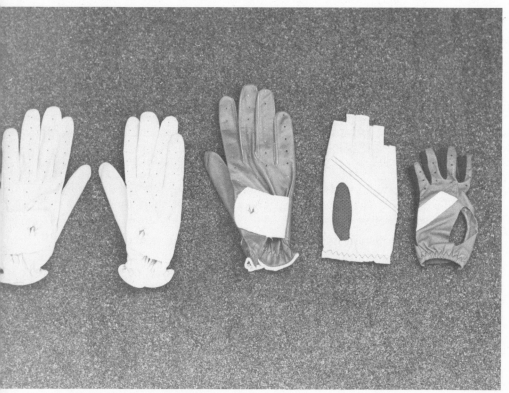

Fig. 14.4 Golf gloves

Shoes

1. Heels should be low or flat—tennis or golf shoes may be worn.
2. Golf shoes (Fig. 14.5) may be purchased at pro shops, department stores, or shoe stores.

   A. Leather or waterproof shoes are good.

   B. Synthetic materials are practical; however, be sure that they fit properly in the beginning as they will not stretch.

   C. Remember that you walk approximately three to five miles on an average golf course in 18 holes. It is essential to have shoes that fit well. Take extra care in selecting your size and width. When being fitted, wear the same kind of socks or footlets that you will wear on the course.

Fig. 14.5. Golf shoes

Hats

1. Sizes and varieties are plentiful (Fig. 14.6).
2. Direct summer sun can be quite strong. Consider the size, shape, and areas you want to cover. A hat can be really useful for keeping your head cool, shading your eyes, or for keeping you dry in rainy weather.

Fig. 14.6 Golf hats

Clothing

1. Generally, men wear long and colorful slacks or shorts and bright short-sleeved shirts.
2. Women wear skirts, dresses, shorts (longer lengths), culottes, or slacks. Blouses are light colored and short sleeved or sleeveless for coolness. Knits are comfortable. Although nylon and dacron shells are feminine looking, they tend to be hot in warm humid weather. Sweaters, wind breakers, and rain jackets with roomy sleeves are comfortable.

Bags

1. Golf bags come in a wide range of sizes and shapes (Fig. 14.7).
2. Personal choice is paramount. Consider the following.

   A. How will you carry it?

   B. How many clubs will it contain?

   C. Will you store shoes and jackets in it?

   D. How many ball pockets do you want?

   E. Is it easy to handle?

   F. Is the material of good quality and is the stitching good?

   G. Does it have space for an umbrella, towels, and other extras?

   H. Does it have a hood to protect your clubs from rain or travel damage?

   I. Can articles be locked in it?

   J. Is the bag the right size for your clubs?

   K. Is its balance good? Will it stand by itself? Is the sling or strap comfortable when you carry it?

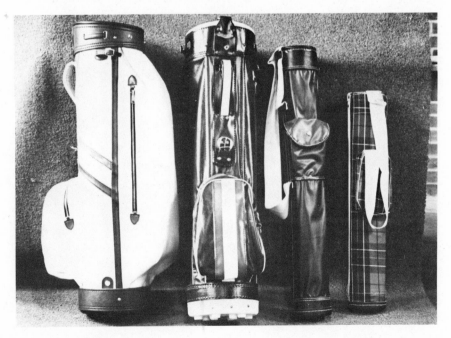

Fig. 14.7 Golf bags

Fig. 14.8 Headcovers

Headcovers

There are various types of headcovers, several of which are shown in Fig. 14.8.

1. *For Woods*
   A. *Leather Headcovers:*
      i) usually come in 1, 3, 4, and flag (or optional number);
      ii) are available in a variety of colors to match accessories or for personalizing;
      iii) are high quality and long lasting;
      iv) retain moisture inside cover—should be allowed to dry thoroughly to avoid prolonged moisture on woods;
      v) are usually the highest in price of all headcovers.
   B. *Knit Headcovers:*
      i) come in 1, 3, 4, and optional wild-card cover;
      ii) come in a variety of colors and usually have large, colorful pompoms attached;
      iii) are easy to take off and put on;
      iv) allow moisture to dry quickly;
      v) are in the medium-price range;
      vi) may be personalized.

C. *Plastic or Synthetic Headcovers:*

    i) come in 1, 3, 4, and optional cover;

    ii) are available in a variety of colors;

    iii) are durable and of good quality;

    iv) retain moisture longer than other types—special care must be taken to ensure they are thoroughly dry to avoid moisture on woods.

    v) are usually the least expensive.

2. *For Irons and Putter*

A. Headcovers for irons and putters are optional accessories. They are used as a matter of preference to keep the clubs from being nicked and from bumping against one another while in the bag;

B. They are available in sizes to fit the various clubs and come in a variety of materials, mostly synthetics.

Carts

1. *Pull Carts:*

A. *Clubsters* (Fig. 14.9)—A clubster is a cart which has a built in bag with a separate compartment for each club. If damaged, replacement of the whole unit is necessary.

Fig. 14.9 Clubsters

B. *Cart only* (Fig. 14.10)—Make sure wheel base is appropriate to balance your chosen bag. Check wheel size—bigger wheels are easier to pull. Check for protective covers that will keep sand and dirt out of the ball bearings. Consider how easily it collapses for storage.

C. *Carts with seats*—Check for weight limits, sturdiness, balance, and ease of handling.

2. *Electric Carts* (Fig. 14.11) Most are rented at the clubs, however, some clubs encourage private ownership. Check differences between gas and electric carts. Check storage features.

Fig. 14.10 Golf cart

Fig. 14.11 Electric cart

3. *Maynard Carts* Robot cart carriers that follow radio signals or beams that are given off by a small device worn by the player. The robot cart follows the person all over the course and stops when the signal is turned off (around the greens and such).

Mats

1. *Indoor or outdoor practice:*
   A. *Coca mats* are inexpensive; have good texture and feel for hitting; good sizes are available; shedding is excessive.
   B. *Rubber mats*—thickness varies; feel is harsh; are very durable; don't shed.
   C. *Astro turf*—is expensive; has excellent texture; feel is excellent for hitting, sound is harsh, is light to carry, wear is excellent.
   D. *Carpeting*—is inexpensive; has good texture. Placing a rubber surface under it helps it hold to the surface better during the hit. A ball may be teed on a rubber tee that is inserted from under the mat through a slit in the surface.

Wet Weather Equipment

1. *Waterproof shoes* These are especially constructed for use in wet weather and are usually made of rubber.
2. *Rain jackets and pants* These can be bought as a whole outfit; combinations of jacket and pants, or jacket and skirt are adequate. Check for full freedom in shoulders for swing. Check to see that material does not rustle or make squeaking sounds when you swing.
3. *Umbrella* These vary in size and colors. Material should be quick-drying and adequate to cover you and caddie. Avoid steel shafts which could attract lightning. Wooden shafts tend to warp. Fiberglass umbrellas are excellent.
4. *Hats and all-weather gloves* Hats should have a large enough brim to keep rain off of the face and glasses. Cotton gloves absorb moisture. Several glove manufacturers have a special all-weather glove that is excellent under rain conditions.
5. *Towels* Carry one on your bag to clean clubs and keep grips dry. Carry extra towels (both large and small) when it is raining.
6. *Hood for bag* Keep hood in the pocket of your bag to cover your clubs in case of rain.

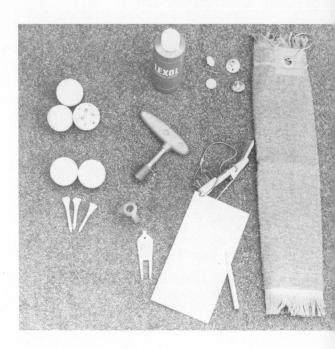

Fig. 14.12 Miscellaneous
accessories

Miscellaneous

The following items are shown in Fig. 14.12.

1. *Ball markers* Small dime-size markers are available. They are sometimes attached to glove fasteners, ball marker pins, etc.
2. *Divot fixer* This is a fork-pronged tool available to repair divot marks.
3. *Spike wrenches* These are a tool to tighten shoe spikes.
4. *Resin* Resin is available in pro shops. It is used to keep grips from slipping.
5. *Leather conditioner* This helps keep leather grips clean and soft.
6. *Bandaids, gauztex* These can protect hands from becoming sore during long periods of practice.
7. *Brushes* These are used to clean faces of irons and shoes.

Care of Equipment

1. *Clubs*

   A. Wash grips with saddle soap, then treat with lexol, resin, or castor oil.

    B. Clean faces of irons with steel wool or stiff brush.

    C. Clean woods with soap and water—then wax.

    D. Never store in damp or wet area.

2. *Balls*

    A. Store in a cool place.

    B. Keep clean during play.

    C. Don't play with scarred balls.

3. *Gloves*

    A. Dry out before storing.

    B. Store in jar or plastic container.

4. *Shoes*

    A. Keep spikes clean and replace lost ones.

    B. Clean shoes and store with shoe trees in them.

15
Learning Aids

Much of our current knowledge about the minute details of the golf swing has been obtained in the past decade through the use of advanced photographic equipment. It is now commonplace for you, on any given weekend, to have the television cameras give you not only instant replay of a well-executed golf shot, but also replay it in such beautiful slow motion that even an untrained eye can see the prime moves of these great swings. Certainly these cameras and their almost commonplace use have aided our game tremendously. Whether you are working with your own individual game or with someone else's, make every possible use of these fine devices. At any stage of development and learning, it is always refreshing to see ideas presented in a novel way. If you can employ some of these ideas in your study, it will often cut the study time down considerably. A picture does what thousands of words could never accomplish.

Loop Films

1. Films can be obtained for 8mm or super 8mm loop projectors.
2. National Golf Foundation and the Athletic Institute have complete sets of films including the following:

   A. Full Swing;

   B. Grip-address Routine;

   C. Short Approach—Pitch;

   D. Pitch and Run;

   E. Uneven Lies.

   These films are available for rent or for sale.

Film Strips

1. 35mm film strips are also available from the National Golf Foundation. They cover the following subjects:

   A. The Game;

   B. Getting Set to Swing;

   C. Building Control into Your Swing;

   D. Getting onto the Green;

   E. Putting;

   F. Courtesies and Etiquette.

   These films can be either rented or purchased and are constantly being updated.

16mm Motion Pictures

1. Many of the leading sporting-goods firms have a variety of films covering many phases of golf. Companies like Shell Oil make their films available, at no cost.

2. The National Golf Foundation has the following Educational Series available:

   A. Welcome to Golf;

   B. Building Your Golf Swing;

   C. Pitching, Pitch and Run, and the Sand Shot;

   D. Putting;

   E. Courtesy on the Course.

   These films are available in a series or by the single film. They may be either rented or purchased.

3. Additional film *lists* are available by writing to The National Golf Foundation, Room 707, Merchandise Mart, Chicago, Illinois, 60654.

Homemade Series

1. Make your own series.

2. Check your own swing on a "before" and "after" basis.

3. Such films can be put to any number of uses besides your own personal use—such as training groups, safety programs, dissertations, and study programs.

Television Replay

1. Television replay is in common use at schools, driving ranges, and private clubs.
2. There is considerable variety in sets—stop action is a big advantage for study purposes.
3. Individuals can run the replays at their own convenience to study special parts of the swing.
4. This can provide exceptionally good study programs.
5. Team members may find them of considerable value for intense indoor winter use.

Sequence Cameras

1. These are excellent for studying various phases of your swing. Usually they take eight sequential pictures.
2. They help when you compare your swing to that of the experts.
3. Most are able to capture the entire swing, as well as many small parts or isolated portions of the action.
4. They provide an exceptional way to compare your beginning swing with later results as you progress and improve.
5. The majority are used with Polaroid film.

Computer Golf

1. Game is played in conjunction with computer centers.
   A. At most of the computer centers that program games, a course is laid out for the player. He selects the clubs for the shot described. His results are returned on the basis of a table of probability for his skill level.
2. Commercially Automated Golf:
   A. Pictures of the shot flash on a screen in front of you.
   B. You may choose from a variety of courses.
   C. Then, in sequence, you play different holes of the course as they appear on the screen; your shot is recorded on an electrically measured surface.
   D. These centers are located in major cities and resort areas.

Visual Aids

1. Wall charts of the rules are available through the National Golf Foundation.

2. Separate pages of the various phases of the swing are also available through the Foundation.

3. Suggestions for emphasis points in the swing are effective in scrapbook form—make your own scrapbook.

4. Diagram rules and course analysis provide better understanding of the subject.

Miscellaneous

1. There are a great many gadgets available that serve as useful practice aids.

   A. Weighted head covers for swing practice with heavier club—available at pro shops;

   B. Swing Image mirror—Swing Image Corporation, 329 Commonwealth, Louisville, Kentucky, 40200;

   C. V.V. teaching grip—Wittek Golf Range Supply Company, 3650 Avondale Ave., Chicago, Illinois, 60618;

   D. Sound rod—Swing Tip Company, 112 Parkview Terrace, Newark, New Jersey;

   E. Putting stroke device—"Putt Trac" Golf, Inc., P.O. Box 2741, Orlando, Florida, 32802;

   F. Mac-Col ball—Bucol Mfg. Company, 1017 S. Locust Street, Oxford, Ohio, 45056; (ball rebounds to roll across feet when hit into wall from 15 feet).

2. Music can be played to accompany the swing, such as:
   A. "Hello Dolly,"
   B. "Down by the Old Mill Stream."

3. Standard Mats:
   A. Coca, rubber, astro turf, carpeting.

4. Balls:
   A. Cotton, plastic, on a string, Mac-Col, c/o Dr. Dick Mackey, Miami University, Oxford, Ohio.

Games—Indoor Golf

1. Indoor games can be set up for your own amusement.
   A. Use mats for tees.
   B. Green outdoor carpeting and astro turf can simulate the greens.
   C. Dowel rods in small wooden blocks make out-of-bounds stakes.
   D. Use tumbling mats or blue cardboard to simulate water hazards.
   E. Discs can simulate putting cups.
   F. Small pieces of carpeting for portable fairway should be placed under plastic balls to protect the floor.
   G. Cut thin foam rubber into the shapes of traps.
2. Lay out as many holes as you want.
3. Make up scorecards.
4. Make up foursomes; use extra players for caddies.
5. This is a fun way to learn the rules and courtesies.

Games in General

1. Use games to review rules and such during your spare time.
2. Have "Spelling Bee" type of elimination on rules, etiquette, and such, for league meetings.
3. "Galloping Golf Game" can be purchased at book and game stores.
4. "Thinking Man's Game"—A "3M" Sports Game.

16
Coaching Suggestions

As a student of the game, you must realize the role of your coach or professional. The professional and coach have many functions to perform to produce successful individuals and golf teams. The coach should be able to set up a good communication system so that he can reach you and all of his players. He should know the game of golf well because he is dealing with top golfers in the area and in the school. A coach or professional must be on friendly terms with his students to enable them to perform at their top skill. He should know each individual's characteristics so that he can help them as individuals and be able to combine them as a team to get the best results. He should know the emotional levels as well as the skill level of each player. As a professional and coach, he will set up reasonable rules and make sure the players follow them. Through coaching, players should build character and learn to be good winners as well as gracious losers. The professional and coach has to be a mother, father, teacher, psychologist, referee, player, and friend, all rolled into one, to produce successful players or a smooth running golf team. Check your overall plan to see that you have a well-rounded program.

Preseason Training

1. Geographical locations determine the type of program needed.
    A. In the South, you can play regularly.
    B. In the North, a supplementary training program should be set up.
2. Set up an overall program and follow it.
    A. Schedule practices.
    B. Schedule exercises and drills—Work on overall body conditioning as well as on building specific muscle groups.
    C. Plan goals for course practice.

D. Compile reading list.

3. Exercises.

   A. Strengthen your left hand and left side.

   B. Squeeze a rubber ball.

   C. Do isometric exercises.

   D. Swing a training club or two clubs at the same time.

   E. Use weights, carefully, to strengthen your forearms, wrists, and hands.

   F. Walk and run—build strong legs.

   G. Swim, ride bicycles, and use exercise machines.

4. Indoor Hitting.

   A. Use plastic balls, Mac-Col hard rubber balls, and driving nets.

5. Read books such as the following:

   A. "The Power of Positive Thinking"—Peale;

   B. "Psycho-Cybernetics"—Maltz;

   C. "The Search for the Perfect Swing"—Cochran & Stobbs;

   D. professional golfers' books, such as those written by Hogan, Palmer, and Nicklaus.

6. Watch televised golf matches and then discuss the plays with your instructor, coach, and golf friends.

7. Listen to strategy talks regarding:

   A. course analysis;

   B. hole analysis;

   C. match and stroke play strategy.

8. Discuss advanced techniques and psychological aspects.

9. Work with video and sequence cameras.

Practice

1. Practice every day.

   A. Exercise;

   B. Hit balls with a purpose;

   C. Use every club in your bag;

   D. Practice from different spots on the course.

   E. Try different types of shots including shots from the sand, shots from the rough, putts, and others.

2. Think, talk, and sleep golf—practice mentally.
3. Warm up before the rounds.
    A. Go to the range.
        i) Hit short chip shots with short irons.
        ii) Work to a full swing with woods.
        iii) Finish with a few short chip shots.
    B. Go to the green.
        i) Chip a few shots to the green.
        ii) Putt.
            a) Start with the tap putt—one inch, then two inches, then three inches.
            b) Go to the longer putt.
            c) Finish with a short one inch putt.
    C. Build your confidence so that you are ready for the round.

Instructing and Coaching

1. Be receptive to the ideas and plans of your instructor and coach.
2. Follow the program your instructor or coach formulates.
3. Keep in good physical condition.
4. Play golf often.
5. Work with a partner so that you can help each other.
6. Play in all kinds of weather.

Mental Approach

Although golf is physical, after a certain level of skill is acquired, the mental aspects become very important.

1. Build confidence in your game and yourself!
2. Practice mentally to improve your physical moves.
    A. Play the course mentally—envision well hit shots to specific areas.
    B. Mentally practice with *each* of the clubs in your bag.
        i) Create the feel of a long, straight, well hit drive.
        ii) Mentally try to create the gentleness needed to hit a soft wedge.
3. Think positively!

4. Envision your shots before you hit them.

5. Set up a realistic par.

   A. When you shoot in the 60's, use a par of 7 for each hole—63 on nine. Keep your score by over or under your 63 par.

   B. When you shoot in the 50's, use 6's for your par.

   C. When you shoot in the 40's, use 5's for your par.

   D. Don't set your goal so high that you are unable to feel any achievement. Learning should be fun, too!

6. Plan your strategy and discuss it.

7. Be alert to every situation:

   A. Changing weather conditions;

   B. Playing conditions.

8. Know your opponents' game.

   A. Know their strong and weak points.

   B. Know their temperament and personality traits.

   C. Knowing these, learn to concentrate on your own game regardless of how your opponents play.

9. Take the game you have that day and play with it.

   A. Have playing thoughts and practice thoughts.

   B. Practice the physical swing on the practice range.

10. Play with golfers who play better than you do.

11. Play with your coach or professional and ask questions as to why shots react the way they do and what clubs, type of shots, angles into greens, etc. should be used.

   A. Talk over situations on the course.

   B. Discuss how you feel about shots.

   C. Try to envision the good shot positions on the course; don't just see the hazards.

Play as Partners

1. When you play with a partner, know your partner's game.

   A. Play together often.

   B. Know each other's strengths and weaknesses.

   C. Help each other with club selections.

2. Pick a partner whose game is similar to yours.

   A. Make sure your strong points complement each others.

3. If you are a steady player, play with another steady player. If you are a scrambler, pair yourself with a scrambler.

   A. Analyze your plays.

   B. Know when to play for the safe shot.

   C. Know when to gamble and take the measured chance.

   D. Plan holes together.

   E. Think alike—think as one!

Team Responsibilities

1. When you play as a team, work as a team.

2. Help each other. Play together and give each other suggestions on positions, clubs, wind, type of shot.

3. If you are the last man on the team, you can win just as many points as the top man, so pull together.

4. Take responsibility for your own equipment, its repair, and for any extras that you need for a given day.

5. Check to see when your practice sessions are scheduled.

   A. Be on time.

   B. Take responsibilities for team duties.

   C. Follow instructions.

6. Remember that your behavior reflects on your group, both on and off the course.

7. Practice good sportsmanship.

8. Be neat in your appearance at all times:

   A. Dress appropriately for the game and the course;

   B. Wear comfortable clothing. Make sure that your hair, fingernails, and such, will not interfere with your swing.

17
Your Golfing Future

Competition

Competition is the natural outgrowth of an improving golf game. It usually starts with a friendly challenge at your local course or among your weekend group. Then, before you know it, you've entered the club championship. As you continue, you progress through your districts, state, and then to national competition. Competition is the great challenge of pitting your game against the rest of the field. Learn to do it with emotional control, good sportsmanship, and the ability to never lose sight of the prime goals of enjoyment and the fun of meeting other people.

Left to right: Jean Ann Johnstone; Patty Berg, L.P.G.A.; Jorgene Barton; Vee Ann Van Patten

Types of competition for various age levels and types of tournaments

1. *Club level:*

   A. *Juniors*

       i) Ages 5 to 18

       ii) Club tournaments and weekly events

       iii) Parent and child team events

       iv) Inter-club matches.

   B. *Women and Men*

       i) Ladies' weekly events, men's weekly events

       ii) Invitationals at home course or other courses

       iii) Handicap events—Your handicap represents approximately your average score over par; handicaps are used as equalizers that enable poorer golfers to play with better golfers in various events.

       iv) Club championships—usually by flights

           a) best eight to sixteen players

           b) flights A, B, C, and D.—Flights are formed by classifying players into groups of eight or sixteen. Individual groups can then compete at their own levels.

       v) Senior Women's and Men's events for people over age 50.

       vi) League play—Teams of six to eight members represent club in matches against other clubs.

   C. *Mixed Events—Many Types*

       i) Men and women as teams or partners

           a) best ball events, alternate shots, handicap, Calcuttas;

       ii) Husband and wife events

           a) club teams playing against other club teams—late evening leagues, twilight leagues, dinner dodgers, etc.

2. *City or District*

   A. *Juniors*

       i) Juniors usually play in city events:

           a) by age groups;

           b) girls and boys separately;

           c) teams represent city against other cities, clubs against other clubs.

B. *Men and Women*

    i) *City championships*

        a) Stroke play is sometimes used to determine positions. In flights, sometimes stroke play alone is used.

        b) Match play may follow during the week.

    ii) *Handicap tournaments*

        a) Regular play stroke or match using handicaps

        b) Team play—two-man or four-man teams

    iii) *Intercity*

        a) Numbers on the teams can vary.

        —Teams play against other cities—score as a team.

3. *State*

A. *Juniors*

    i) Pee-wee Tournaments

    ii) State Juniors—by age groups

B. *Men and women*

    i) State Championships

        a) These include match play, stroke play, or a combination of both.

        b) Entries for competition are limited by handicap.

    ii) Best ball team play—one state against another

    iii) Mixed events—husband and wife (or male and female)

4. *National*

A. *Juniors*

    i) District qualification

    ii) Divisions by ages

    iii) National Junior Tournaments:

        a) United States Golf Association sponsored handicap and area elimination

        b) Other sponsors for Juniors, such as Jaycees, Western Golf Assoc., etc.

B. *Men and women*

    i) Women must have a low handicap to enter

        a) A handicap of six or less is required for the bigger ones —National Amateur, etc. Some require sectional qualifiers.

    ii) Men require district and then sectional qualification for the major amateur tournaments.

    iii) Major national tournaments for amateurs

        a) National Amateur

        b) Western Amateur

        c) Trans-National

        d) North and South Amateur

        e) Florida Winter Circuit

    iv) Major open and amateur events for professionals and amateurs

        a) United States Open

        b) Title Holders

        c) United States Senior Events

        d) Masters Tournament for Men

        e) Foreign Championships.

5. *International Events*

  A. *Women's*

    i) *Curtis Cup Matches* (international team matches)

        a) These include the six to eight top amateur players in the country, specifically those who have compiled the best tournament records over the past two years.

        b) They are played against the top six to eight players from the British Isles.

        c) These matches are played every two years alternating sites between England and the United States.

    ii) *World Cup Matches* These matches take the best Curtis Cup players and team them against France, Britain, and Italy.

  B. *Men's*

    i) *Walker Cup Matches* (International team matches)

        a) These matches consist of the best six to eight amateur players. Playing records are compiled from best amateur records over the past two years of amateur events. The matches are played alternating years in the United States and British Isles.

    ii) *World Cup Matches*

        a) Players chosen from Walker Cup matches compete against British Isles, France and Italy.

iii) *Ryder Cup matches*

a) Top American professional male golfers compete against top professionals from Great Britain.

6. *School Events*

A. *Boys and Girls—high school—governed by interscholastic rules*

i) Teams–four to eight players.

ii) Interscholastic Spring or Fall matches:

a) District

b) Year-end District and State Tournaments —some by school size; others regardless of school size

B. *Intercollegiate*

i) *Men and women*

a) Six to twelve members are chosen by skill.

b) This team plays against other teams in district or league.

c) Invitationals—Other colleges in general area are invited to compete.

d) Districts—Teams of certain areas play one another, such as Midwest, Central, North-South, and Big Ten.

e) National Intercollegiate Matches sponsored by N.C.A.A. and A.I.A.W. (Association for Intercollegiate Athletics for Women).

—men representatives of different sections

—women, no handicap limit, represent school

—individual play

—team play

two-man (woman)

four-man (woman).

Future Careers

A variety of careers are available to the skilled, knowledgeable golfer. It is impossible to discuss each one in great detail in this book. Qualifications should include a love of the game, enjoyment of meeting people, liking somewhat irregular working hours, and the ability to organize yourself. Listed on the following pages are some of the opportunities that you might investigate.

1. *Teaching in a high school or college:*

   The United States Golf Association allows a teacher to be compensated for golf instruction as long as the time spent does not exceed 10% of his or her teaching hours. Amateur Standing is not forfeited under this rule. Teachers in public schools must meet certification requirements of the State in which they teach.

   A. *Secondary schools—Junior High program*
      i) Introduce golf into the classroom.
         a) Include the whole picture.
         b) Be strong on rules and courtesies.
         c) Keep students busy with all parts of the game.

   B. *High School*
      i) Make golf mandatory for the individual sports program for the Juniors and Seniors.
      ii) Encourage freshmen and sophomores to get started.
      iii) Encourage development of individual programs.
      iv) Sponsor golf teams.

   C. *College*
      i) Golf should definitely be a part of the program.
         a) Offer golf all seasons of the year.
         b) Emphasize the social carry-over.
         c) Point out its strong aid to physical fitness.
         d) Stress the enjoyment to be gained.
      ii) Start and encourage teams.
         a) Allow these teams to represent your college in competitive events.
         b) Use them as a tool to teach good sportsmanship.

   D. *Summer Camps*
      i) Camp counselors who give golf instruction as part of their compensated duties are *not* amateur golfers.
      ii) When looking for available areas, use the surrounding fields.
      iii) Try to get some type of green surfaces—Use carpeting, indoor-outdoor carpeting, towels, sand greens, astro turf, etc.
      iv) Use indoor facilities.
      v) Develop the social and emotional aspects of the game.

2. *Recreation*
   A. YMCA-YWCA Professional
      i) Add golf to total year-round programs.
         a) Give group lessons, about 15–20 people per group.
         b) Give winter and spring sessions.
         c) Develop leagues for summer play.
         d) Have inter-Y play and competition.
   B. *Industrial*
      i) Teach groups of 15 to 20 per class.
      ii) Hold winter as well as summer sessions—indoor and outdoor.
      iii) Form leagues—encourage play at all levels:
         a) Junior—boys and girls;
         b) Men and Women—mixed and individual;
         c) Senior—mixed and individual.
      iv) Hold tournaments—all types and for all age groups.
   C. *Hotel and resort areas*
      i) Run tournaments. Organize events.
      ii) Organize mixed group activities.
      iii) Hold conventions—organize events.
      iv) Run driving and putt-putt ranges.

3. *Small Golfing Facilities:*
   A. Run indoor driving ranges.
   B. Provide outdoor facilities for day or night driving range.
   C. Miniature golf—daytime and/or nighttime (lighted) facilities:
      i) putt-putt courses,
      ii) courses smaller than par three's, .
   D. Par-three Golf Courses—daytime facilities and/or nighttime (lighted) facilities

4. *Golf Professionals*
   A. Teaching Pro—P.G.A. or L.P.G.A. requirements must be met to become a member. Possibilities include:
      i) Freelancing or working independently
      ii) Becoming head professional at golf club
         a) Running a pro shop
         b) Teaching the members

iii) Assisting head professional

iv) Giving lessons—group and private

v) Conducting clinics

    a) high school

    b) college—undergraduate and graduate

    c) community—group lessons

vi) Coaching golf teams

    a) high school—boys, girls, or mixed

    b) college—assist local schools

    c) club—help them get started in the spring

vii) Running tournaments for club members

viii) Assisting at golf leagues and tournaments

    a) Working with other pro members to help area committees run tournaments—being available to act as referee

    b) Encouraging golfers of all levels and skills

ix) Working with community projects

x) Promoting junior golf

    a) Assisting with local programs to see that the juniors have a sound set-up,

    b) Giving clinics in the spring to encourage play,

    c) Organizing events with parents and other age-level juniors;

xi) Working for National Golf organizations.

B. Touring Professional (P.G.A. or L.P.G.A.)

  i) Must meet P.G.A. or L.P.G.A. standards to join the tour

  ii) Plays in professional tournaments to earn a living

  iii) Travels constantly

  iv) Competes against the world's greatest players

  v) Gives clinics and/or exhibitions for manufacturers of golf equipment

  vi) Acts as public relations representative for golf supply houses while on tour

  vii) Does commercials for manufacturers on television, etc.

  viii) Teaches golf during off-season of tour

Touring is highly expensive—expenses usually run over $15,000 per year including tournament entry fees, caddie costs, housing, and travel.

C. Teaching Professional

    i) Teaching pros are generally the same as regular professionals except that they may assume that the greater part of their time will be spent teaching rather than in the areas of management and merchandising.

5. *Miscellaneous Occupations*

  A. Work for sporting goods companies

    i) Promotion and sales

  B. Work for manufacturers that deal with any kind of golf supplies

  C. Sell golf clothing

Glossary

Glossary

Ace—a hole played in one stroke—hole-in-one

Address—the position taken just before hitting a shot, which includes readiness of grip, stance, and body position

Amateur—a person who plays golf as a sport and does not accept money for prizes

Approach—a short shot taken to the green, usually within 50 or 60 yards from the pin

Apron—the short grass bordering the green

Away—refers to the position of the player's ball that is farthest from the flag

Back spin—the spin imparted to the ball which causes it to slow down or to bounce back when it lands

Ball—a golf ball that meets U.S.G.A. standards of size, weight, and acceleration

Banana ball—slang name for a sliced shot

Berm—another name for the apron or edge of the green

Best ball—a term used to describe a game in which a twosome or a foursome play as a team and only the best ball score is recorded

Birdie—a score that is one stroke under par

Blast—a sandtrap shot in which the club makes contact with sand behind and under the ball

Blind bogey—an event in which the player selects a number to be added to or subtracted from his 18 hole score that will net him a score usually between 70 and 80. The score closest to the "blind" score wins.

Blind hole—a green that is hidden from view as you approach it

Bogey—a score that is one stroke over par

Brassie—an old term used for a number 2 wood

Bunker—a depressed or raised mound of earth, usually with sand in the depression or on one side of the mound

Bye—a term used in tournaments when a player has a pairing with no opponent for that round

Caddie—a person who carries a player's bag and who may give advice to the player

Calcutta—team events sponsored by a group that takes bets on the winners and other team placements.

Carry—the distance that a ball is airborne from the club to the spot where it lands

Casual water—a puddle or water that is not intended to be a water hazard; definitely a temporary condition

Chilly dip—to hit fat or behind the ball and have the ball dump a short distance

Chip shot—a short approach shot with a low trajectory

Club head—the whole lower part of the club that is intended to make contact with the ball

Collar—edge around green, often called apron, fringe, or berm

Course rating—a rating in strokes of the playing difficulty of a course. The rating, done by an outside association, establishes the difficultness of the course so that handicaps between different courses can be standardized.

Cup—name for the hole that contains the flag on the green

Cut shot—a shot, made with a lofted iron, that follows an outside to inside club-head path to the intended line of flight and produces much backspin

Divot—a piece of sod that is cut away from under the ball at impact

Dog-leg—a hole that has a bending fairway to the left or right

Dormie—when a player or side of a match is as many holes up on the opponent as there are holes left to play

Double bogey—a score that is two strokes over par

Down—the number of holes that a person or side is behind in the match

Draw—a ball that travels *slightly* to the left of the intended line of flight with a rather straight trajectory not a dramatic curve

Drop the ball—the player faces the hole and drops the ball over his shoulder, then plays it from wherever it comes to rest

Dub—to miss a ball to such an extent that it rolls along the ground

Duffer—the name given to a poorly skilled player

Eagle—a score that is two under par for the hole

Explosion—another term given to the blast shot from a sand trap

Fade—a ball that travels *slightly* to the right of the intended line of flight with a rather straight trajectory not a dramatic curve

Fairway—closely mowed area between the tee and the green

Fat—a swing that is made at the ball but has its contact point well behind the ball

Flag stick—the stick that marks the location of the hole on the green

Flight—the division of players in a tournament

Flight of ball—the line of flight or path of ball

Fore—the warning word called out loudly that means "Look out—a ball is coming in your direction—*duck.*"

Forecaddie—a person who is sent out ahead of the golfers to watch where the balls will land on long shots

Four-ball—another name for best ball competition when four players form a team or are matched

Fringe—another word used to describe the apron or outer edge of the green

Frog's hair—the outer edge or apron around the green that has been allowed to grow long and matty

Gimme—a slang name for a very short putt that it is assumed that the player can make. In a sense he is asking the other players to "give me" the putt without hitting it into the cup. It counts as a stroke.

Grain—the direction that the grass grows on the green

Grass cutter—a low, hard-hit ball that skims the grass

Green—the putting surface

Gross score—the total number of strokes used to play 9 or 18 holes

Ground under repair—marked area that is temporarily unfit for play

Grounding the club—placing the sole of the club on the surface

Halve—to tie a hole in score as two fives or two sixes, etc.

Handicap—a percentage of the average score that you shoot over par

Handicap strokes—the numerical ranking of holes on a given course with 1 representing the hardest hole on which to make par and continuing to 18 which represents the easiest; a hole upon which player receives handicap allowance

Hazard—a term that covers bunkers, water, ditches, and such that require special rules for play

Heel—the back part of the sole of the club

Hole high—ball coming to rest, even with the pin

Hole out—to finish putting out by hitting the ball into the cup

Honor—the right to go first when hitting. On the tee, this is determined by the person scoring the lowest score on the previous hole; on the first hole, this can be determined by a flip of a coin.

Hood—to close the club face at address

Hook—a ball that has been hit and curves to the left of the direction intended

Hosel—that part of the club above the neck where the shaft meets the club head

Lie—the position of the ball on the turf or other surface

Lie of club—degree of upright angle of club when club is soled

Links—another name for the course

Lip—the edge of the cup

Local rules—those rules made to apply only to a specific situation on a specific golf course

Loft of club—degrees of vertical angle of face of club—such as straight driver or angled 9-iron

Loose impediment—those pieces of gravel, cut grass, and twigs that impede the execution of the shot

Lost ball—ball that is not found after five minutes of search

Marker—objects placed on the teeing area to show where the ball should be placed to start play on the hole:

1. tee—on the tee as above
2. hazards—designated boundaries of course and hazards
3. small coin-like object placed behind ball before removing ball from putting surface

Marker—a scorer, in competition, who records score

Match play—two sided hole-by-hole competition; one team or person wins when they are ahead by more holes than the number of holes remaining to be played.

Medal play—competition in which the total number of strokes is counted. When extra holes are played, the player who scores the lowest score on the extra holes is the winner (also called stroke play).

Medalist—the person scoring the lowest gross score on the first day or round of a tournament

Mulligen—allowing a provisional ball to be played only on the first hole and the choice of taking a second try without penalty; for use in friendly games—never used in competition

Nassau—a competition in which three points are scored, one for the winner of each nine and one for the winner of the total eighteen

Neck—the curved part of the club head where the shaft joins the head

Net—a score after the handicap has been subtracted

Nonamateur—see professional.

Obstruction—artificial, man-made objects on a golf course, such as fences, water fountains, benches, and shelters

Out-of-bounds—that area off of the club property or marked by white stakes from which there may be no play

Overspin—forward spinning of the ball

Par—the number of strokes a good player should score on a hole; determined only by the length of the hole, not its difficulty

Partner—a player associated with another on the same side in a competition

Penalty stroke—a stroke added to your score for an infraction of the rules

Pin—another name for the flag

Pitch shot—a short shot that has a high trajectory and rolls a very short distance after it lands

Preferred lies—improving the position of the ball as in winter rules

Press—in betting, to double the bet at any time

Press—to force the shot beyond its normal limits

Professional—a person who willingly receives compensation for teaching, playing, or participating in some phase of golf. Compensation includes accepting prize money over $200.00 per prize and certain expenses not acceptable to the U.S.G.A.

Provisional ball—a second ball hit when there is a doubt whether the first ball has gone out-of-bounds or is lost

Pull—a ball that is hit to the left of the intended line of flight—not a dramatic curve

Punch shot—a half shot, firm and directed, usually with lower trajectory than is normal for the club

Push—a ball hit slightly to the right of the intended line of flight—not a dramatic curve

Qualifying round—the first round of a tournament when the player's score is used to rank him numerically with the other players

Rain maker—slang for a ball hit high into the air—skied ball

Rim the cup—when the ball circles the cup without dropping into it

Rough—that part of the course where the grass has been allowed to grow longer than the fairway areas

Rub-of-the-green—conditions that denote that the ball must be played as is, as the breaks fall

Sand trap—another name for bunker; depressions that are filled with sand

Scratch handicap—having no handicap—plays par golf

Scorer—the person who marks the score on the card. Score must be verified by the player.

Shaft—that part of the club that lies under the grip and attaches to the club head

Shank—a ball that is hit off the neck of the club and goes directly to the right at almost a 90° angle to the intended line

Sky—to hit the ball very high with little distance

Slice—a ball that has been hit to the right of the intended line to the target in a dramatic curving circle

Snake—to knock in a long, long putt

Stance—the position of the feet at address

Stance (closed)—right foot drawn back

Stance (open)—left foot drawn back

Stance (square)—toes parallel to the target line

Stick—another name for the flagpole

Stiff—hitting the ball very close to the pin

Stroke—any attempt to make contact with the ball

Stroke play—competition in which the total number of strokes is counted. When extra holes are played, the player who scores the lowest score on the extra holes is the winner.

Sudden death—a tied match after playing last hole; additional holes played until one player wins

Sweet spot—hitting the ball flush on the center of the face of the club

Target—intended spot or hole where the ball should land

Tee—the peg that is placed under the ball to hold it off the ground; or an elevated teeing area that denotes the start of the hole

Texas wedge—using the putter off the edge of the green

Through the green—that area of a golf hole from the teeing area including the surface all the way to the cup.

Toe—the part of the club at the front tip or front portion of the face of the club

Top—to hit the ball on the top half, causing the ball to roll along the ground; hitting high on the ball

U.S.G.A.—United States Golf Association, the standard setting association for golf in the United States

Underclub—to misjudge or not take enough club for the distance needed

Unfit ball—a ball that is damaged to such an extent that it is unfit for play

Unplayable ball—a ball deemed by the player to be in such a position that he does not want to play it

Up—to be holes ahead of your opponent in match competition: 1 up, 2 up, etc.

Waggle—the back and forth or nervous wiggling of the club and the player's body while preparing to address the shot

Whiff—to make an attempt to hit the ball and miss completely; the stroke still counts

Winter rule—another name for preferred lies when the player is allowed to make small adjustments to the lie of the ball in the fairway or on the fringe of the green